CUBA

TITLES IN THE MODERN NATIONS SERIES INCLUDE:

Canada
China
Cuba
England
Germany
Italy
Mexico
Russia
Somalia
South Korea

MODERN
NATIONS
—OF THE—
WORLD

CUBA

BY MARY VIRGINIA FOX

LUCENT BOOKS
P.O. BOX 289011
SAN DIEGO, CA 92198-9011

Acknowledgment
I would like to acknowledge the help given to me by Henry Schroeder of Schroeder Publications. He is past president of the Wisconsin Newspaper Association and state chairman of the National Newspaper Association.

Library of Congress Cataloging-in-Publication Data

Fox, Mary Virginia, 1960–
    Cuba / by Mary Virginia Fox.
       p.   cm. — (Modern nations of the world)
    Includes bibliographical references and index.
    Summary: Discusses the discovery, history, geography, people, and culture of Cuba, its strategic location and importance, and its significance in the world today.
    ISBN 1-56006-474-9 (lib. bdg. : alk. paper)
    1. Cuba—Juvenile literature.   [1. Cuba.]   I. Title. II. Series.
F1758.5.F69   1999
972.91—dc21   98-36882
                                          CIP
                                          AC

Copyright © 1999 by Lucent Books, Inc.
P.O. Box 289011, San Diego, CA 92198-9011
Printed in the U.S.A.

Contents

INTRODUCTION   6
  A Strong Influence

CHAPTER ONE   9
  Discovery

CHAPTER TWO   18
  The Look of the Land

CHAPTER THREE   27
  Spanish Control

CHAPTER FOUR   40
  Free at Last

CHAPTER FIVE   52
  Castro Has His Way

CHAPTER SIX   69
  The Culture of Cuba

CHAPTER SEVEN   80
  Cuba Today

  Facts About Cuba   95
  Chronology   97
  Notes   101
  Suggestions for Further Reading   103
  Works Consulted   104
  Index   106
  Picture Credits   111
  About the Author   112

INTRODUCTION

A STRONG INFLUENCE

The great influence that Cuba has had on world affairs is out of proportion to its small geographical size and population. Today some 9.6 million people call the island home, but before Europeans came to claim the land, it is doubted that there were more than 1,000 or 2,000 inhabitants.

Cuba is a curved sliver of land in the mouth of the Gulf of Mexico, 746 miles long and from 25 to 125 miles wide, and it is located less than 100 miles from Key West, Florida.

A VULNERABLE AND VALUABLE LAND

It is Cuba's strategic location that has always made the country vulnerable and valuable to other countries. In the early days, when ships sailed from Europe to the New World, Cuba's ports were the stopping points for ships needing to replenish supplies and for trade. Ships patrolling Cuba's waters controlled traffic to the rich treasures of Central and South America.

The island nation was coveted by Spain, France, England, Holland, and Portugal. Even Thomas Jefferson thought of claiming Cuba to protect the newly formed United States from foreign invasion. During the twentieth century, Communist Russia sought Cuba's alliance, which nearly brought on a war involving all the countries of the world.

Cuba has been ruled by kings and dictators, and its citizens have never known complete democratic freedom. The country's history reflects a time of wealth, when pirates ruled the seas and Cuba served as their treasury, followed by years of poverty and near starvation.

Then came other eras of prosperity with foreign investment. In the 1920s Cuba's capital city, Havana, hosted tourists from around the world as they came to enjoy luxurious hotels, elegant gambling casinos, and white sand beaches. Yet only a few Cubans were able to profit from the luxuries enjoyed by outsiders.

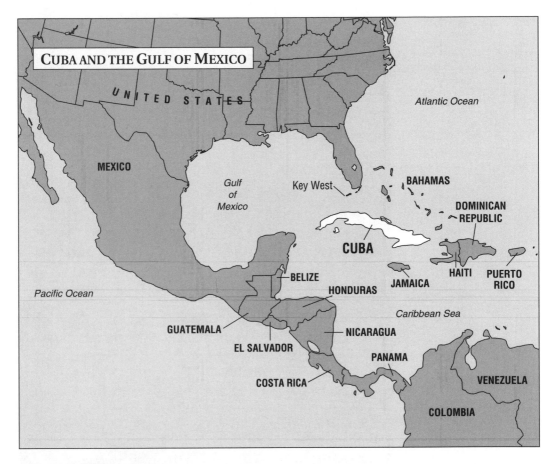

CUBA AND THE GULF OF MEXICO

UNITED STATES

Atlantic Ocean

MEXICO

Gulf of Mexico

Key West

BAHAMAS

DOMINICAN REPUBLIC

CUBA

Pacific Ocean

BELIZE

HONDURAS

JAMAICA

HAITI

PUERTO RICO

Caribbean Sea

GUATEMALA

NICARAGUA

EL SALVADOR

PANAMA

COSTA RICA

VENEZUELA

COLOMBIA

CONFLICTING IDEOLOGIES

Cuba is a country of conflicting ideologies. Cubans have always resented foreign intervention, even though their island does not have enough resources to support itself, such as fuel and mineral resources for modern industry. As a result, the country was ripe for revolution.

Two strongmen stepped into the role of leadership. First there was Fulgencio Batista y Zaldívar, who took over the government with military force but promised to adopt a democratic constitution. Batista's constitution was a remarkable document that guaranteed human rights and government responsibility to bring about a peaceful end to civil war. Within five years, however, graft and thievery returned. The final revolution to bring about peace was led by Fidel Castro, who has established himself as supreme dictator for nearly half a century.

Fidel Castro has been the patriarch of Cuba for over fifty years. Even after the fall of so many Communist govern-ments, Castro remains firm in his belief in the system.

While many Cubans believe the promises given in Castro's fiery speeches and his claims that the country is better off under exacting government control, many others have fled the country to save their lives if not their property.

Today Cubans are a mixture of races and colors: mulattos with black and Spanish ancestry; mestizos with Indian and Spanish blood; and criollos, whites born in Cuba. There are also minorities of French and Chinese ancestry. Cuba is a country of diversity held together by the firm dictatorship of Fidel Castro. Although the quality of life has improved among the poorer classes, the nation's citizens have lost their individual freedom. What the future may bring is hard to guess.

DISCOVERY

1

Christopher Columbus set sail from Spain on Friday, August 3, 1492, to map a route to India and China. These fabled lands had been visited by Marco Polo two hundred years before when he journeyed from the East. Tales of great wealth urged Columbus to find a shorter trade route to the rich lands.

Almost immediately, heavy seas pounded the three small vessels in his fleet. Provisions were washed overboard, and sails on the largest ship, the *Santa María*, strained and split in ragged strips. The *Pinta* and the *Niña* floundered in mountainous seas and were almost lost.

The only known land to the west on their meager map were the Canary Islands, which were considered to be the edge of the world. To save his little fleet, Columbus ordered all three ships to put into shore for repairs and to obtain additional supplies of water and food.

A month passed before Columbus and his crew were prepared for another attempt at discovering the westward passage to the wealth of the Orient. Day after day the ships sailed into the unknown. The crews threatened mutiny, but Columbus pointed out that they had passed floating grasses in the sea and that twice birds had circled the masts of the ships. These were certain signs that land lay ahead, and Columbus urged them not to give up within sight of their goal. They had no way of knowing, however, that their goal was actually thousands of miles away on the other side of the world.

LAND HO

Finally, at two o'clock on the morning of October 12, Rodrigo de Triana, a sailor on lookout, sighted land. The crew rejoiced as the ships dropped anchor. Columbus stepped onshore and knelt to give thanks to God, naming the land San

9

CHRISTOPHER COLUMBUS

Christopher Columbus was born in Genoa, Italy, in 1451. His father was a weaver with no ties to a sailing life, but boys who lived close to the harbor that was filled with tall ships and sailors with exciting tales of adventure often headed for a life aboard ship. Columbus went to sea as a young boy and claimed to have traveled as far north as Ireland, England, and Iceland before he headed across the Atlantic.

Columbus died on May 20, 1506, penniless and without glory in his own time. He had not found the gold he was after, but he will always be remembered as the first person to find a passage to the West Indies and return. His discovery led others to follow, so that the New World became part of the European world.

Christopher Columbus set out for India and China only to discover Cuba and the New World.

Salvador. But in the distance he could see other islands, which he thought were off the main coast of India.

Sails were again set, and they continued their search for signs of human life and a good anchorage. Fifteen days after the first landfall, they reached the northeastern coast of what is now Cuba. No one is sure of the exact location of this historic site, but Columbus wrote in his journal that he "anchored in the mouth of a river, in water surrounded by green trees, flowers, and sweetly singing birds." [1]

What he had found was a long ridge of land jutting from the sea, low in some places, but with two mountain ranges.

HUMAN CONTACT

Columbus described the people he found in this new land as well formed and handsome, with brown skin and straight black hair. "They are the best people in the world and above all the gentlest. . . . They became so much our friends that it was a marvel," [2] he wrote.

Although the inhabitants wore few clothes, what they did wear, particularly the necklaces around their necks, was of great interest to Columbus. Excitement mounted when he and his crew saw the gold nuggets used as decorations. Surely if the ruler of this country was rich enough to give gold to simple fishermen who lived in thatched huts, mind-boggling riches were certainly not far off. When Columbus tried to ask them where the gold came from, they pointed inland toward the mountains that rose from the coast and said "Cubanacan."

By coincidence, their country's name sounded like the name Kublai Khan, the all-powerful ruler who Columbus had heard controlled great wealth in the Orient. Kublai Khan was indeed a ruler in Asia, but he was certainly not the powerful chief on this island in the Atlantic Ocean. Yet all of this was unknown to the explorer from Spain.

Columbus searched the coasts for the rich cities he had read of, but only small villages of palm-thatched huts were found. He traded glass beads and little brass bells for fruit and gold nuggets, then he left to explore other islands. Before

A Cuban cacique, or chief, greets Columbus and his men. Columbus was thrilled by the sight of the natives' gold necklaces and jewelry.

he left Cuba, he persuaded five young Indian men, seven women, and three children to come aboard the ship. He hoped to teach them the Spanish language so that he could find the answers to the all-important questions about the geography and wealth of the area. The experiment was a failure. The native Indians rebelled. Instead of being punished, they were released on yet another island in the chain that seemed to stretch across the entire horizon.

LEFT BEHIND

Columbus continued to search the horizon, but his men were becoming impatient and threatened mutiny if a return voyage was not planned before the weather worsened. A near-fatal storm struck on Christmas Day 1492, and the *Santa María* was wrecked off the coast of Hispaniola, an island smaller than Cuba. Today this island is shared by two countries, the Dominican Republic and Haiti.

No lives were lost, but now a decision had to be made. There was not enough room on the remaining two vessels to transport the combined crews back home. Columbus left the men of the wrecked ship on the shores of this smaller island with express orders to make friendly contact with the natives and discover their gold mines.

The thirty men who remained did little to promote friendly feelings. They quarreled among themselves and

Columbus's ship, the Santa María, *runs aground off the coast of Hispaniola. The Spaniards who remained on the island after the wreck were killed by the Indians.*

stole women from the Indians. By the time Columbus returned on his next voyage, the Indians had rebelled and killed every one of the Spaniards.

These original settlers had built barricades and had started to fortify the shore. A shredded Spanish flag was found in the ruins. It was here that the next arrivals landed and again set out to possess the land. They brought with them two Catholic priests, who had come to convert the Indians to Christianity. The big island of Cuba was where they started their preaching.

CUBA'S FIRST INHABITANTS

Two very different groups of people lived in Cuba when the Spaniards arrived. Since both cultures were primitive and lacked a written language, little is known about them. Records contain only what was reported by the Spanish.

The major group was the Tainos, who are also referred to as the Arawak. They were natives who originated in Central and South America and migrated to the string of islands known today as the Antilles, perhaps as long ago as 3500 B.C.

THE FLEET OF DISCOVERY

The caravel *Santa María*, the flagship of Christopher Columbus's fleet, was only 128 feet long with a 26-foot beam (width). Its capacity is estimated at 100 tons, and it carried a crew of 56 men.

The *Pinta*, under the command of Martín Alonso Pinzón, was half the size of the *Santa María*, and the *Niña* was even smaller. The captain of the *Niña*, Vicente Yáñez Pinzón, was the brother of Martín Alonso.

In contrast, the tonnage of U.S. aircraft carriers of the *Nimitz* class is set at 104,240 tons. The length of such ships is 1,092 feet. Columbus's three ships would have taken up very little space on a four-and-a-half-acre flight deck.

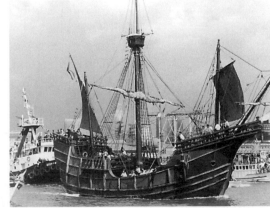

In a 1991 reenactment, a replica of Columbus's Santa María *leaves Spain.*

The Tainos lived in small villages, each governed by a chief they called a cacique. The Tainos cultivated corn, yams, and yucca, which was pounded into a powder and used as the base for cassava bread.

They spun coarse thread or twine from a type of wild cotton, which they made into hammocks for sleeping. This was also the cord used for fishing lines and nets. They made nothing of metal. Their fishhooks were of horn and their harpoons were tipped with bone. Their principal weapon was a wooden spear that was used for hunting rather than warfare. At one time deer, rabbits, squirrels, and several species of small wildcats were prevalent.

The Tainos also hollowed canoes out of huge logs and used the crafts for fishing and for traveling great distances between neighboring islands. In a territory where fierce hurricanes were a seasonal hazard, the Tainos had learned to forecast the weather by studying natural cycles and cloud patterns.

MEN OF THE ROCKS

The second and smaller cultural group was the Carboneys, which means "men of the rocks." At one time it is supposed that they occupied the whole of Cuba; by the time the Spaniards arrived, however, their numbers had decreased. Their demise was probably caused by their inability to cope with a more advanced race of people.

Most of the Carboneys lived isolated at the far western end of the island. They made their homes among huge rocks and in caves. Their entire diet consisted of wild fruit and fish, and they did not practice any form of agriculture. They had not learned to make tools of bone or stone, and their implements consisted of shell fragments and wood. The Carboneys did not survive long after the Spaniards arrived. Archaeologists have found few of their remains.

OTHER ADVENTURERS

A race of white men had come to inhabit the land. Word that there were new worlds to conquer spread fast. In 1508 another Spanish sailor, Sebastian de Ocampo, became the first explorer to sail all around the coast of Cuba, proving once and for all that the land was truly an island. This was not the great mainland of the Far East, but it was a promising land.

Ocampo also discovered the harbor of Havana, which was deep and well protected from storms.

Between 1492 and 1511, the Indians, as they were called by the Spaniards, were aware of the tall ships that entered their waters. During the stormy season the Indians stayed close to shore in their dugout canoes, but the big ships tried to ride out the winds. More than one met their fate as they broke up on reefs. Some lucky sailors, clinging to timbers, were able to swim to shore. They joined others who had ventured from Hispaniola to explore Cuba. Instead of being grateful that they had been welcomed by Cuban Indians, they set about putting their own warlike set of standards into practice. Their passion for gold set them against the people who had befriended them on first arrival.

THE FIRST FIGHT FOR SURVIVAL

The Indians from Cuba heard disturbing news from the nearby island of Hispaniola, where the majority of the "white giants" had gathered. Some of the Indians there had chosen to flee their homeland and seek shelter on the larger island of Cuba. The stories they told of enslavement and torture were puzzling and frightening.

WIND AND CURRENTS

Once Columbus showed the way, others followed. The Caribbean was an easy sea to enter but a difficult one to leave. The northeasterly trade winds blow month after month at a steady fifteen to twenty-five knots, varying little more than a compass degree in direction. The ocean currents help the wind. Waters from the Atlantic Ocean push over the coral shelf guarding the northeast coast of Cuba.

Then the river of water turns northward to drive through the channel between the Yucatán Peninsula into the Gulf of Mexico. Warmed by the tropical weather, the current sweeps along the southern coast of Cuba and squeezes through the ninety-mile strait between Cuba and Florida. From then on the Gulf Stream hugs the North American coastline before angling back toward Europe.

Once the ocean had been tested of all of its vagaries, all traffic followed the same course. Havana was the last port of call for a direct voyage back to Spain.

A chieftain, or cacique, named Hatuey watched helplessly as his people were forced to dig for gold and to wash the sand from riverbeds in search of the glittering metal. They were killed if they did not obey, and their wives and daughters were often taken by the Spaniards, who had not come with women of their own.

Hatuey was determined to free his people from the cruel Spaniards. He had heard the loud explosion of their guns. He knew his people could not match the enemy in weapons, but he resorted to what magic he had. According to an account of a Spanish missionary, Hatuey held up a small basket filled with gold nuggets.

He called on his people to dance around the magic pebbles for which the Spanish were willing to kill. They danced until they were exhausted. Then they threw all the gold into the river. They hoped this would prove that they did not treasure such trinkets and the Spanish would see how worthless the metal was. They could not know how much these strangers valued the gold specks that washed up on the sand. There was no turning them back.

FULL-SCALE INVASION

The full-scale Spanish invasion that Hatuey had so feared came in 1511. The Spaniard Diego Velázquez set sail from the colony on Hispaniola with the intention of setting up his own

TRIAL AND EXECUTION

Hatuey was Cuba's first freedom fighter. The battles were unsuccessful, but his legend of heroism is told in Cuban schools today.

Hatuey was captured and tried as a heretic in front of a jury of Spanish priests and soldiers. Enough words had been learned so that a halting communication took place. According to the priest who recorded the event, Hatuey was told that the doors of heaven would be open to him if he would tell the secret of the source of their gold.

"Do Spaniards go to heaven?" Hatuey is supposed to have asked.

"The good ones do," the priest replied.

"Then I will not go there. I do not want to spend eternity in any heaven filled with Christians."

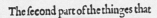

kingdom. The Spaniards landed on the southeastern shores of Cuba, near present-day Baracoa, and began building a fort guarded by a strong stockade.

The work had barely started when Hatuey and his band of guerrillas attacked with spears. They suddenly appeared from ambush, killed two Spaniards, and wounded several others. The soldiers opened fire in return, but by then Hatuey's warriors had disappeared.

Three more times Hatuey's men attacked, but they could not protect themselves from two strange weapons the Spaniards had brought with them to the New World: horses and dogs. It was the bloodhounds that brought about the defeat of the Indians. They could not hide.

Few natives survived the early years of conquest by the Spaniards. The Indians died, worked to death as slaves or as victims of diseases the white man brought with him.

Little gold was found in Cuba, but the newcomers from Spain discovered a land rich in other resources. Here was a land free for the taking, where settlers from Europe could grow food and crops for trade. Sugar and tobacco would make some rich.

A woodcut from the seventeenth century describes the virtues of the tobacco plant, which made many of Cuba's Spanish settlers rich.

2

THE LOOK
OF THE LAND

Today geologists know that the land we call Cuba was gradually raised from the seafloor some 20,000 years ago by pressure from the shifting of continental plates. The main island of Cuba rests on a shelf of rock 300 to 600 feet below the surface of the water, from which the various cays (coral islands) and coral reefs arise. The long, narrow island extends some 746 miles from east to west, about the same distance as New York to Chicago. At its widest point it is only 125 miles from coast to coast. The average width is a mere 62 miles. On a clear day Cuba can be seen from the town of Key West on the southern tip of Florida. Less than a hundred miles separate the two countries.

The Cuban archipelago has a combined area of 42,804 square miles (110,861 square kilometers). At last count, it included some 3,700 islets and cays, some no more than sandy uninhabited beaches.

JOINED TO THE MAINLAND

At one time Cuba was connected with other islands of the Antilles chain as well as the mainland of Central and South America. The mountains of southern Cuba are formed from the same kinds of rock as southern Mexico, Jamaica, and the Yucatán Peninsula. Earthquakes continue to reshape the land.

Except for the steep cliffs of the Sierra Maestra range that plunge into the sea, most of the Cuban shoreline is fringed with coral reefs. In the north, an almost unbroken line of small cays guard the shore. In the south, the largest of the islands is the Isla de la Juventud, once called the Isle of Pines.

Cuba is one of the least mountainous islands in the area, although one of its peaks in the Sierra Maestra range reaches 6,540 feet. The average elevation of Cuba is no more than 300

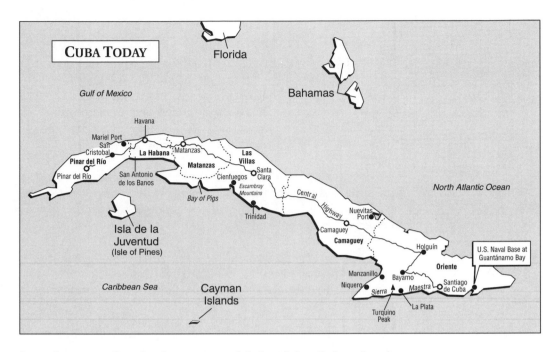

CUBA TODAY

Florida

Gulf of Mexico

Bahamas

Havana

Mariel Port
San Cristobal
Pinar del Río
Pinar del Río

La Habana Matanzas

Matanzas

San Antonio
de los Banos

Cienfuegos

Las Villas

Santa Clara

Escambray
Mountains

North Atlantic Ocean

Bay of Pigs

Trinidad

Cent*ral*

Highway

Nuevitas
Port

Isla de la Juventud
(Isle of Pines)

Camaguey

Camaguey

Holguín

U.S. Naval Base at
Guantánamo Bay

Caribbean Sea

Cayman
Islands

Manzanillo

Niquero

Oriente

Bayamo

Sierra

Maestra

Santiago
de Cuba

La Plata

Turquino
Peak

feet above sea level. Almost two-thirds of the Cuban land-scape consists of flatlands and rolling plains.

RIVERS AND SHORELINE

Most of the country's more than two hundred rivers originate in the interior near the island's watershed and flow northward or southward to the sea. Smaller streams and gullies remain dry, except during the rainy season when heavy flooding is common. Most rivers are not navigable, and hydroelectric power is only now being considered to produce energy for manufacturing plants. There are no large natural lakes, although Lake Hanabanilla was artificially created in the early 1960s. It is surrounded by beautiful hills, one of the most scenic of the island's regions.

Cuba's approximately twenty-two hundred miles of coastline have some of the world's finest harbors, deep and well protected. There are about two hundred in all.

Coastal swamplands dotted with mangroves also mark the shoreline. The largest swampland area covers more than seventeen hundred square miles. The soil here is poor for growing crops, but on higher ground many types of plants are harvested. Beans and corn are important staples. Even rice is grown in areas where freshwater can flood the fields. Citrus

SINKHOLES

The Cuban landscape does not have much soil erosion because of the flatness of the land, but there are numerous sinkholes. These occur because of the substrata of limestone rock, which has been worn away by underground streams. Caves are frequent, and when the roof of a structure wears away close to the surface, the ground collapses, leaving a hole.

Some caves are still expanding as the limestone edges on the surface continue to crumble. Some are deep enough to swallow a three-story building. These strange features convinced the early Spaniards that they had discovered abandoned gold mines.

Today two caves, Cueva de los Indios and Cueva de Bellamar, are open to the public. Beautiful limestone formations with stalactites and stalagmites make them popular tourist attractions.

fruit is a commodity that is often exported, but sugar and tobacco are by far the most important crops.

WILDLIFE

There are approximately seven hundred species of mammals, reptiles, amphibians, and birds on the island of Cuba. At one time deer, rabbits, wild pigs, squirrels, and several small species of wildcats were prevalent. Much of their native habitat has since been converted to farmland, and few remain.

The Zapata Swamp remains one of the most extensive habitats for Cuban wildlife. Most of the area has been designated a national preserve. All but three of Cuba's native birds breed here. Two of these birds, the Zapata wren and the Zapata rail, are found no other place in the world. This is also the nesting place of the world's smallest bird, the Cuban bee hummingbird. Parakeets and parrots flash color from tree to tree, and in other areas, flamingos add their own splashes of pink.

The swamp also remains one of the last strongholds of the Cuban crocodile. Although a small variety of python is found in parts of the island, there are no poisonous snakes native to the land.

The deadliest predator is a much smaller creature. The climate and the setting make this a great place for the breeding of mosquitoes. Health officials are constantly on guard to eliminate new outbreaks of malaria and yellow fever.

TREES

The sabal palm dominates part of this swamp-filled wilderness. It is a true survivor, able to exist in poor soil and withstand hurricane-force winds. It can live for more than one hundred years and reach heights of seventy feet. It is topped with a spoke of fifteen to thirty fronds, each of which is up to six or seven feet long. These fronds are harvested to make weatherproof thatched roofs. It is against the law to cut these trees or their fronds within the Zapata Swamp preserve because it destroys the nesting places for the birds.

Among the most valuable timber native to the island are mahogany, cedar, and West Indian ebony. All are used for making fine furniture.

The sweet-smelling white mariposa, or butterfly jasmine, is the national flower and was often worn as a symbol of patriotism during Cuba's wars for independence. Cubans have a reason to feel proud of what the land offers.

WEALTH FROM THE SEA

Cubans can also take pride in the wealth from the sea. Early Cubans used the harvest from the sea to add to their diet. Today people from around the world have come to recognize that the waters off the Cuban coast are a paradise for sportfishing. The warm waters support a variety of fish, including snapper; tarpon; emperador, or swordfish; bonito; barracuda; mackerel; marlin; and several varieties of shark. The tortuga, or sea turtle, and the manatee, or sea cow, are both on the endangered species list because of overhunting in the past.

Fishing has always been a major source of food supply. In the past the average fisherman went out for a day with nets or hooks in a small dugout canoe and returned with a bounty for his

An island nation, Cuba harvests fish, shellfish, lobster, and sponges (pictured).

Workers cut sugarcane, one of Cuba's most profitable commodities.

immediate family. Oysters, crabs, crawfish, and a spiny lobster are all harvested for food.

CLIMATE

The ocean's warm current helps moderate the climate so that balmy weather prevails. Seasonal average temperatures range from sixty-six degrees Fahrenheit (eighteen degrees Celsius) to eighty-six degrees Fahrenheit (thirty degrees Celsius), but the humidity is often high. The rainy season runs from May to October, and dry weather prevails between December and April.

Cuba's location makes it prone to fierce tropical storms, especially hurricanes, some with winds over 150 miles an hour and heavy rains of up to 11 inches in a 24-hour period. September and October are the worst months for storms.

In 1993 almost all homes along the southeastern coast of Cuba were leveled and trees were uprooted. Many lives were lost, and no crops were harvested for more than a year.

SUGAR IS KING

Despite its severe and sometimes devastating storms, Cuba's climate and soil conditions are favorable for growing sugarcane. It is a crop that requires an extensive use of human labor and large tracts of ground. Cane must be cut at a certain height from the ground and in a certain way to ensure proper growth for the next season. A sugarcane plant may continue to produce for up to fifteen years, although nowadays growers realize that rotation of crops brings higher yields. Modern machinery has been developed for some harvesting, and the sugar mills of today are huge, complicated factories.

Sugarcane from the fields is transported directly to mills that crush the cane to produce the juice that is called *guarapo*. The juice is boiled at high temperatures to produce *melado* or molasses. This heavy brown liquid is forced through enormous centrifuges that spin the syrup into sugar. Raw sugar is dark brown, thick, and moist, and it must be further refined to become plain white sugar.

MOSQUITO CONTROL

It was not until the beginning of the twentieth century that an attempt was made to control the pesky mosquito. A Cuban doctor named Carlos Finlay theorized that yellow fever and malaria were caused by the mosquito. At the turn of the century, Dr. Walter Reed from the U.S. Army medical team became interested in the theory and decided to test the idea.

Two special huts were constructed. One hut was made mosquito proof, but the inside of the dwelling was made deliberately filthy. Sheets that the men slept on were from the very beds of those who had died from the disease.

The second hut was kept scrupulously clean, but mosquitoes were plentiful. It was here that the volunteers became ill and some died. Now the work of destroying the breeding ground for the mosquitoes took full priority. Ditches and pools were drained or covered with an oil film. By the end of 1901 the number of mosquitoes in Havana alone was cut by 90 percent and the incidence of yellow fever was reduced accordingly.

U.S. Army doctor Walter Reed.

Another important by-product of sugar is high-quality rum. The Spaniards were the first to export this commodity when they ran out of gold.

Other by-products are also produced during the processing of sugar. The fiber left from the original crushing of the cane can be used as fuel or made into paper. Newspapers in Cuba are actually printed on sugarcane.

FAVORABLE BALANCE OF TRADE

Sugarcane is still the most valuable cash crop for Cuba, and the prosperity of the country fluctuates with its yield. Drought and hurricane damage have been known to bring devastation and near starvation for much of the population of Cuba, but when a bumper crop of sugarcane is harvested, everyone prospers. Prices of all goods hinge on the exchange rate of what is exported to other countries. A favorable balance of trade means that most other goods are plentiful. If Cuba can sell its produce, it has enough money to buy other needed items.

During the first step in the refining process, sugarcane is crushed to produce the juice called guarapo.

Today farming specialists are trying to diversify crops for home use and international trade so that one poor sugar crop harvest will not bring such a swing in prosperity. Other crops grown for export are coffee and cocoa, which grow in the mountainous regions. Although Cuba is over 60 percent lowlands, the richness of the soil on the hillsides makes both products profitable.

When French and British immigrants first came to the island, they established coffee plantations. Today little cocoa is grown, but high-quality coffee is Cuba's favorite nonalcoholic beverage.

Rice, corn, bananas, and a large variety of vegetables are harvested both for the local markets and for export. Cuban families also raise more exotic items, such as mangoes, guavas, coconuts, papayas, and avocados.

CIGARS

Tobacco has been the second most important agricultural crop for Cuba. This is a product native to the land. When Columbus arrived, the Indians were seen smoking bundles of rolled up leaves.

Today high-quality tobacco is grown in Cuba. It is a crop that requires a lot of labor, not machinery, but it takes fewer acres under cultivation to grow a cash crop. This means that farmers with small plots of land can compete with large farms.

FIRST AGRICULTURE

The early settlers of Cuba, the Tainos, shared property communally and cultivated simple crops of corn and beans. Even before the Spaniards came, the forests had an abundance of tropical fruit.

Today country people near Baracoa can walk a few hundred yards into the woods and find cocoa, oranges, papaya, mangoes, coconut, and almonds to eat; fibers from which to weave cloth; and many other useful products.

Although the Tainos were not used to eating meat in quantity, wildcats and birds were often hunted and, with the abundant supply of marine wildlife at their shores, these early people were living a life of plenty in a tropical paradise when Columbus arrived.

The tobacco leaves must be cut at a precise time when they are at full maturity. If left in the fields too long, they become tough and strong in flavor. After they are cut they are tied in small bundles to be hung to dry in a ventilated shed. When they reach the exact degree of dryness, they are rolled into cigars. Cigarettes can be machine-made, but not the expensive Cuban cigars prized the world over.

It takes practice to roll a quality cigar. These skilled laborers are called *torcedores*. One by one the leaves are put on a wooden block and rolled with the palm of the hand. An unusual tradition has evolved over the course of years. These workers are entertained by readers, called *lectores de tabaquería*. The readers must have strong voices to be heard in the large factory rooms that house from four hundred to five hundred workers.

The second most important agricultural product in Cuba is the cigar, which is hand-rolled in factories like this one.

CATTLE

Not all land is cultivated; some is kept for pasture. The cattle industry has always been important in Cuban history. Spaniards brought the first cattle with them on their ships. With plenty of open range, the herds quickly increased.

Leather processing has become an important side market for ranchers and Cuba is known for its shoe industry.

Today dairy products are available in areas where there is refrigeration. In the big cities, milk and cheese are easily available but are quite expensive.

MINERALS AND OTHER RESOURCES

Cuba's main mineral resource is nickel. Nickel accounts for about 96 to 98 percent of all mineral exports. The output of the three largest processing plants is about 100,000 tons annually.

Output of iron and crude steel averages 320,000 tons, but manufacturers hope that this figure can be greatly increased so that the country can reduce the amount of imported material from Japan. Cuba has produced copper at the Matahambre mines in the Pinar del Río province for over 70 years. More recently, discoveries of deposits containing lead, zinc, chromate, and cobalt have been reported; however, these minerals are found in small quantities and would not significantly help the balance of foreign trade accounts.

To balance its national budget, Cuba relies on its agricultural resources rather than its manufactured products. The balancing act has often been hard to accomplish. There are shortages of goods and the price of many items, including food and housing, are high. There are no millionaires in Havana today, but there are no beggars on the streets either.

Spanish Control

3

When the Spanish gave up their search for gold on the island of Cuba, they found it in Mexico and Peru, the land of the Incas and Aztecs. Early Spanish settlers rushed to the mainland to get their share. Instead of the population of Cuba growing, it lost many of its permanent residents to Mexico and beyond. The Cuban settlers who had held on to the land they had cleared, however, were ready to make a profit.

Havana was the strategic port of call for all ships heading back to Europe. Returning ships were forced to swing by the southern coast of Cuba to catch the current that would help them on their way back to Europe. The task of transporting treasure to the countinghouses of Seville was a hazardous one.

PIRATES

In the early days of the Spanish Main, sea captains warily searched for the safest route home. As pirate ships began to funnel away the profits of trade, the captains recognized the virtue of banding together in flotillas of ships to protect each other. By the mid–sixteenth century, Havana was the port where the captains gathered to make up their convoys. Treasure ships began to forest the bay with their towering masts as they waited for weather conditions to improve and the arrival of Spanish men-of-war ships sent as military protection. Crews, soldiers, and passengers had to be fed and housed, and they spent their money in Havana while waiting.

Local Cubans now had a guaranteed market for their wares. Their early produce consisted mainly of meat from the cattle they raised and the hides that were thus provided. Timber, especially the beautiful mahogany wood, was cut and piled on decks for export. But there was more, much more, they could sell. Rum turned a great profit, and there seemed to be no better place to grow the necessary ingredient, sugar, than on the surrounding fields.

A Spanish galleon plies the seas. Cuba became a main port for Spanish ships traveling from the New World back to Spain.

POPULATION GROWTH

Profits brought a wave of immigration. By 1760 there were more people living in Havana than in New York, Boston, or Philadelphia, and the city boasted a great many cultural accomplishments. The University of Havana had been built in 1728, and by 1734 Cuba had a police force. The first newspaper was published in 1763, and the next year Cuba established a national postal service that eventually served all of the Americas. A public library came next, and the first theater, Teatro Tacón, was built. It is the oldest theater in continuous operation in the Western Hemisphere. In the midst of all this growth, war was about to come to Cuban soil.

UNDER ENGLISH RULE

During the profitable seventeenth century, Spain had its own battles to fight. In 1762, with Spain and England at war in Europe, the English navy assembled a force of two thousand ships and twenty-two thousand men to take over the island of Cuba. Instead of attacking Havana directly by way of the well-guarded harbor, English troops landed in a nearby village, then kept Havana isolated without supplies. The siege ended within two months, when the English took over complete control of Havana on August 12, 1762.

After only a year, however, England gave Cuba back to Spain in exchange for what is now the state of Florida. Under Spanish control, Cuba continued to trade with other nations. The British had developed a particular craving for Cuban tobacco and rum from the surgarcane. As soon as the Spanish discovered this to be such a profitable commodity, royal enforcers stepped in to take control of the trade. No sale could be made except through the intermediary of the Casa de Contratación, an agency that set the price for all exports and took a large percentage of the transaction for itself.

PIRATES WITH ROYAL BACKING

Spain was not the only country that lusted for the wealth pouring into Havana's harbor. Pirate ships waited until the treasure ships were loaded and then set their gun sights. France and Spain had long been at war on the high seas. Now, with the backing of the French government, Jacques de Sores, a French privateer captain, headed for a port in Cuba to plant the flag of France.

He docked at the town of Santiago de Cuba, where he held the whole town for ransom. Encouraged by that success, the next year he headed for Havana. Governor Pérez de Angulo fled, leaving only twenty-six men to defend the town. Later the governor had second thoughts and returned for a night attack, but De Sores rallied his men and drove the Cubans back. Before leaving, he stripped the city of everything of value that he could load aboard his ships and burned what he left behind him.

Pirates celebrate their plunder.

CIVIL WAR BREWING

This caused great concern among the landowners and mill owners, who resented being governed by foreign officials who were sent to Cuba on short-term appointments from the Spanish court. Some officials never bothered to ride out into the fields and check on the crops. They were referred to as *peninsulares*, referring to the shape of Spain.

FORTIFYING THE CITY

During the 1600s Spain was determined to make Havana safe from attack. Two formidable fortresses were built at the entrance to the harbor, El Morro on one shore and La Punta on the other. Chains were strung across the narrow harbor entrance whenever attack was imminent. At first, the chains were made of iron and bronze, but these were too unwieldy; later, logs were chained together to block the entrance.

The walls of the fortresses were built of limestone from nearby quarries. To this day they appear blinding white in the tropical sun. Behind their battlements, cannon were poised to aim at any enemy sail. Few captains, either pirate or those with the blessing of a royal insignia, dared come too close. Only stealthy attacks from across the land were possible, but soldiers guarded the rear as well.

Even today, the well-built fortress of El Morro appears sturdy and intimidating.

The large landowners, most of whom were whites born in Cuba, resented the arrogant way they were treated. Once they even burned their crops in defiance of the laws imposed on them by the *peninsulares.* These landowners felt they had earned the right to control their own land. Secretly they began meeting to discuss ways of gaining independence from Spain.

POWER TO THE NORTH

Like Cuba, the thirteen North American colonies owned by the British also wanted independence. Spain was ready to give aid to the colonies to weaken England's power. At the time of the American Revolutionary War, Spain held Louisiana, Florida, and Cuba, and it allowed New Orleans, at the mouth of the Mississippi River, and Cuba to become gateways through which the American colonies received their war goods.

Spain had not anticipated that the newly formed United States would turn into a power player itself. As early as 1795, talk of war began between the United States and Spain over the possession of Cuba. With the United States poised right on the shores of Cuba, Spain worried about its ability to defend the island and maintain control over shipping between North and South America. Fearing an American attack, Spain formed an alliance with France, in hopes of obtaining help in protecting Spanish interest. For the moment Cuba seemed to be saved for Spain.

To free Haiti from French control, Toussaint-Louverture led an army of black slaves in a bloody revolt.

REVOLUTION IN HAITI

Nearby Haiti was going through its own revolution about this time. Led by Toussaint-Louverture, Haiti's black slaves organized their own army, and the bloody revolt succeeded. Haiti declared itself independent of France in 1804.

Although Cuba's wealthy landowners desired liberation from Spain, their visions of an independent Cuba did not include freedom for the country's slaves. Dating from the mid-1700s, African slaves had provided much needed labor for the sugar plantations. The Haitian slave revolt dampened Cuba's own taste for independence. Spanish troops would be the only protection for Cuba's landowners if their slaves followed Haiti's example. Concern also existed that at some point Spain might force Cubans to abandon slavery.

Although some educated merchants and professionals still hoped for independence, few stepped forward to lead the cause. For some Cubans, a better alternative seemed to be an alliance with the United States or even annexation.

A secret society known as the Rayos y Soles de Bolívar, founded in 1821, supported annexation. Its members hoped that the United States would grant more freedom for local government than Spain offered, especially in regards to slavery. Slavery was still an important part of the economy of America's Deep South. So the Cubans thought they would gain an advantage by being annexed by the United States.

THE MONROE DOCTRINE

Although many U.S. citizens favored the idea of Cuban annexation, American foreign policy made it clear that the United States would take no action in Cuba. This policy was stated by President James Monroe in the foreign policy that was to bear his name: the Monroe Doctrine. In simple terms, the doctrine declared that European nations should stay on their side of the Atlantic, and the rights of Central and South American countries would be protected by the United States.

It defended the rights of newly formed independent nations against foreign interference, but it also acknowledged the rights of Spanish domination over Cuba. Although it sounded like a contradiction in terms, the doctrine stated that the United States was defending the choice that the people of Cuba had made for themselves.

MORE COLONIAL REBELLION

Most of the rebellious sentiment within Cuba was expressed in talk, not in action, until the mid–nineteenth century. In 1851 a small force of rebels led by General Narciso López landed on Cuban shores from the coast of Venezuela. His purpose, he said, was to liberate the country from Spanish rule. It was an inspirational thought, but he had other motives. In particular, he planned to share in the expanded business opportunities by setting up trade monopolies.

The rebel forces flaunted a flag bearing a white star on a red triangle. Three blue stripes and two white stripes made

SLAVERY IN CUBA

Sugar is a crop that requires a lot of backbreaking work. Because Cuba's native inhabitants had all but been killed off in the original search for gold, the Spaniards imported slaves from Africa. The earliest census record available shows that as many as five thousand slaves a year were bought and sold in Havana. The exact number was probably much higher in the whole country.

As cruel as the practice was, life for slaves in Cuba was far better than in the colonies that became the United States. Without slaves, the few white landowners could never have made a livelihood from farming. They had a selfish reason for at least giving some humanitarian consideration to keep a cooperative workforce. The climate was tropical. Landowners from Spain were not used to such grueling physical labor. Slaves were necessary to make the land profitable.

During the sixteenth and seventeenth centuries, slaves in Cuba were allowed to marry in the church, which meant that these marriages were binding by law. No white owner could separate a family, and children born to a black mother were considered free or slave according to a mother's status.

Another law forbade selling a slave for more than the original purchase price, which meant that, although the worth of a trained worker might increase his value, there would be no speculation in further sales.

Some slaves earned their freedom by fighting with their owners to defend the country from pirate attacks. They were then allowed to work as free craftsmen and to own and operate inns, farms, and ranches. In later years many of these privileges were withdrawn.

There was a great deal of intermarriage between blacks and poorer whites and between blacks and Indians who owned land. They became part of the Cuban mixture of races called *guajiros*, or simply peasants, losing the status of slaves.

Black slaves cut and load sugarcane on a Cuban plantation. Although they were not free, Cuban slaves were protected by some laws.

up the right section of the banner, the same design as is used today. The rebels, however, did not find enough local support, and they were badly beaten. General López was captured and executed. His last words were, "My death will not change Cuba."[3] And, indeed, it took many years before change came to Cuba.

THE TEN YEARS' WAR

One attempt to bring change lasted ten years. It began October 11, 1868, when Carlos Manuel de Céspedes and a group of planters from the Cuban province of Oriente (at the island's eastern end) proclaimed their independence from Spain. Although the military campaign was started by property owners, the causes they fought for went beyond the usual interests expressed by the landowning class. If they succeeded, they vowed to abolish slavery. They also stood for representative government and against the power of the Catholic Church, which controlled education within the country. Schooling was not free, and only the wealthy could afford to educate their children. These church-sponsored schools taught subjects that favored the class that supported the church.

Though the rebels had noble aims, their military resources were limited. Even the victory at Bayamo, which inspired a hymn that later became Cuba's national anthem, could not save the rebellion. After ten years of bloodshed and the loss of an estimated 50,000 Cubans and 208,000 Spaniards, a peace treaty was accepted. Under the 1878 Treaty of Zanjón, Spain retained control of Cuba while agreeing to enact reforms.

Reforms were minor, and it was not until 1886 that slavery was officially abolished in Cuba, the last country in the world to do so. Even that event was a hollow victory in some respects. Slaves who were freed had to earn their freedom by working the next eight years for their masters without pay. Many reasons existed for further revolutionary action.

The main complaints against Spanish rule consisted of excessive taxation and an autocratic government that allowed little representation by the citizens. Positions of power were held by Spanish-born citizens, not by Cuban nationals. The basic freedom of speech and the right to hold meetings to make complaints known were also lacking.

THE NATIONAL ANTHEM

The Cuban national anthem, *La Bayamesa*, was composed following the rebel victory at Bayamo. While the Spanish soldiers soon forced a retreat, the song lived on.

Run to combat, men of Bayama
May the motherland be proud of you.
Don't fear a glorious death,
For to die for the motherland is to live.
To live in chains is to live
Under shame and indignity.
Hear the clarion call, to your arms, brave ones, run!
Don't fear the ferocious Spaniards,
They are cowards, whose total tyranny
Can't resist the brave Cubans;
Their empire will fall forever.
Think of our triumphs,
Think of them as fallen;
Because they were cowards they
   ran away beaten,
Because we are brave we know
   how to triumph!
We can shout Free Cuba!
With the terrible explosion of the cannon,
Listen to the clarion call.
To your arms, brave men, run!

JOSÉ JULIAN MARTÍ

José Julian Martí (1835–1895) was the man who put these complaints into words. The son of a Spanish artillery sergeant stationed in Cuba, Martí was fifteen when the Ten Years' War started. He was shocked by the treatment of black slaves on Cuban plantations and felt that the oppressive Spanish-controlled government, which favored rich landowners, should make radical changes to help the conditions of all classes of citizens.

At age seventeen, the idealistic student was arrested for his inflammatory writing. He was put to work on a chain gang breaking up rocks to make street pavement. After finishing his sentence, Martí was deported to Spain in 1871, where he studied law during his exile. He also wrote poetry and essays, which caught public attention in Europe and in the United States.

José Martí fought for Cuba's independence from Spain.

Between 1892 and 1895, Martí devoted himself entirely to the cause of independence for Cuba. While in the United States he founded the Cuban Revolutionary Party, worked to raise funds for it, established a newspaper to further the party's aims, and organized volunteers for an armed return to Cuba. The insurrection order was written and signed by Martí and smuggled into Cuba rolled inside a cigar in 1895.

BATTLE LINES ARE DRAWN

Martí left the military leadership to Generals Máximo Gómez y Báez and Antonio Maceo y Grajales, both survivors of the Ten Years' War, but Martí insisted on being on the battle line as well. Martí and the first six thousand rebels landed in several places in eastern Cuba in February. Fighting was fierce. When they could find no other weapons, Cubans resorted to attacking Spanish cannon with machetes.

Martí was one of the first casualties during the battle at Dos Ríos on May 19, 1895. His death elevated his stature in the eyes of the Cuban people.

Even Spanish generals praised the courage and skill of the "poor people's army," but the Spanish government meant to put an end to the fighting once and for all. The job was given to General Valeriano Weyler y Nicolau, called "the Butcher."

Weyler believed that the simplest way to stem the rebellions was to annihilate the Cuban population. He ordered all inhabitants of the country districts that were outside the fortification lines of the towns to enter the areas occupied by the troops. They were then forced into crowded camps with no sanitation and almost no food. Thousands died of starvation and disease. Weyley almost accomplished his goal by starving people to death.

As one traveler wrote,

> I traveled by rail from Havana to Matanzas. The country outside the military posts was practically depopulated. Every house had been burned, banana trees cut down, fields swept with fire, and everything in the shape of food destroyed. . . . The country was wrapped in the stillness of death and the silence of desolation.[4]

On December 7, 1898, General Maceo, the popular black guerrilla fighter, was killed in action. Now the Spanish government was sure the rebels would realize the hopelessness of their cause and settle for peace. The opposite was true. The harder the Cubans fought, the more praise they received from outside their own country.

SYMPATHY FROM ABROAD

The United States was sympathetic to the plight of the Cubans, but it was also selfishly protecting its own interests. As Secretary of State Richard Olney wrote at the time, "The wholesale destruction of property on the island is utterly

Cuban rebels attack a Spanish fort. Although Spain dealt harshly with the "poor people's army," Cubans refused to give up the fight for independence.

The U.S. battleship Maine *explodes in Havana harbor. The explosion set off a chain of events that led to war between Spain and the United States.*

destroying American investments that should be of immense value, and is utterly impoverishing great numbers of American citizens."[5] Olney gave no mention of the war's impact on the citizens of Cuba.

Spain recognized that the United States was considering armed intervention. To head off this catastrophic event, Spain made many concessions, even granting a democratic government in Cuba. All problems seemed to have been solved. Peace would probably have come if not for the dramatic events of February 15, 1898.

"REMEMBER THE *MAINE*"

The U.S. battleship *Maine* was sent to Havana to protect American citizens there. On February 15 it steamed into the harbor. Shore leave was given to all but 253 crewmen and one officer. Meanwhile, angry crowds lined the docks. The ship's visit was regarded as a threatening gesture to Cuba; however, the crew of the *Maine* went ashore without incident.

During the night the city was awakened by a giant blast that shook stone walls. Flames ripped through the hull of the

Maine. The ship was destroyed and all of the crew still aboard were killed. The cause of the disaster was never discovered. Americans blamed underwater mines, while Spanish investigators insisted it must have been an internal explosion. Anti-Spanish sentiment ran high in the United States. Revenge was the rallying cry.

Blaming Spain, the United States demanded that Spain leave Cuba and pay for the loss of life. Spain refused and declared war on the United States. The U.S. Congress answered in like words. U.S. forces, including Theodore Roosevelt's Rough Riders, invaded Cuba. "Remember the *Maine*" became their battle cry. The war's only major battle, the attack on San Juan Hill, several miles to the east of Santiago de Cuba, came on July 1, 1898. It was a costly battle for both sides. Within six months the war was over, and so ended Spain's four-hundred-year rule over the island of Cuba.

4 FREE AT LAST

In February 1902 Tomás Estrada Palma was elected president of Cuba by popular vote, and on May 20, 1902, the United States announced that the government of Cuba would be transferred to Cuban hands. The prophecy made by José Martí that "the day will come when we shall place on the strongest fort of our country, the flag of the single star," came true. In Martí's words, they had created "a foundation of a just Republic open to all, one in territory, in law, in work."[6] The Cuban flag was raised over the El Morro fortress, which had helped save the country from pirates two centuries before.

In spite of these glowing words, the country's first president had seemingly insurmountable problems. Two major parties existed, and although their names changed frequently, they favored either conservative or liberal policies. The two parties found it impossible to cooperate or compromise. The supporters of both parties were essentially members of the aristocratic class, however. The conservatives were, for the most part, members of the landed gentry. The liberal party was made up of wealthy city merchants. Little thought was given to the common people who had only recently emerged from slavery.

THE PLATT AMENDMENT

The United States recognized Cuba's independence, but with certain reservations. The Platt Amendment, passed by the U.S. Congress in 1901, was added to the new Cuban constitution. It imposed several conditions, including giving the United States the right to lease land for a naval base on Cuban territory. It also gave the United States the right to intervene with military force should events on the island seem to be dangerous to American interests.

Continual political unrest in Cuba led to U.S. military intervention from 1906 to 1909 and again in 1912. This was

cause for great dissent among Cubans, who felt that they were again putting themselves under the control of a foreign power.

During the intervention, the U.S. military government helped to set an honest example for the administering of funds. No longer was the wealth of Cuba sent to a foreign king. Surplus money was available to build roads, sewers, and waterworks. Perhaps the most important accomplishment was the eradication of yellow fever with the cleanup of breeding sites of mosquitoes and the emphasis on sanitation.

Reforms were made in the administration of the University of Havana, the island's major university and the oldest one of the three established for higher learning. Only professors who actually taught courses were to receive salaries. It was discovered that some professors who had earned degrees in Cuba no longer lived in the country but continued to receive payment by keeping their names on the university's faculty list.

Cubans flew their new flag over the El Morro fortress after declaring independence in 1902.

BOOM AND BUST

Other elections followed the 1902 presidential elections, always with accusations of graft and corruption. The prosperity

A 1920 photograph shows sugarcane fields and a refinery at Guantánamo Bay.

of Cuba, however, was closely tied to events in the United States. With foreign money available for investment in Cuban markets, Cuba's financial future looked bright following World War I. As is true today, sugar was Cuba's most profitable export commodity. The United States had a monopoly on accepting Cuban exports.

The failure of sugar beet crops in the United States in the early 1920s caused a sudden rocketing of sugar prices. A wild season of speculation followed. Sugar planters and mill owners borrowed money to clear additional land, and thousands of acres of fine timber were sacrificed.

All too soon the price of sugar plummeted because the market was glutted. Land worth a fortune the previous year could now be purchased for practically nothing. Banks foreclosed on loans, and the treasury of the Cuban government was nearly bankrupt. The National City Bank of New York and the Royal Bank of Canada offered money to bail out the Cuban government, but in return they ended up owning a large portion of Cuban real estate.

There was growing discontent among the populace. Mill-workers and sugarcane cutters were starving while foreign tourists continued to live on a grand scale, enjoying gambling and elegant entertaining. The rift between the living standards of most Cubans and those who came from overseas was huge and troubling.

DICTATOR MACHADO

In 1924 Gerardo Machado y Morales, a skillful politician, was elected president. He was popular at first because he proposed extensive public works projects that gave needy Cubans jobs. To continue his programs, however, Machado raised taxes and borrowed huge sums of money from overseas. At the same time, he funneled large sums of money into a fund to expand the Cuban army, and he placed his friends in important military positions.

To control the country and to eliminate the opposition party, Machado assumed the powers of dictator. The constitution was forgotten. Many students started organizing efforts to oust Machado from power. Riots were frequent, arrests were brutal, and prisons were crowded.

To make matters even more desperate, the Great Depression of the late 1920s and early 1930s affected world trade, nowhere more severely than in Cuba. The price of sugar, Cuba's most important export, hit record lows. This meant that Cuba had little cash to pay for goods that had to be imported.

People were laid off from work, and those with jobs had to wait for their pay. Havana workers called a general strike, which lasted several months and caused more hardship.

BATISTA COMES TO POWER

On September 4, 1933, an army revolt led by Sergeant Fulgencio Batista y Zaldívar succeeded in forcing the resignation of President Machado. This still did not bring about a semblance of order. Ramón Grau San Martín was elected provisional president, but it was Batista who ruled Cuba from behind the scenes.

The Cuban congress launched a number of labor reforms, but with the treasury empty and public employees unpaid for months, the riots continued. Other presidents came and went,

Fulgencio Batista y Zaldívar led a revolt to oust Gerardo Machado in 1933, and later ruled Cuba as dictator.

but finally in 1940 Batista was officially elected president under a new democratic constitution. It was a constitution that gave hope for reform and jobs for all. Batista was rabidly against communism, a stand that gave him support in the United States.

Cuba declared war on Germany soon after the United States entered World War II, presumably trying to gain favor with its American ally. There was little agreement on this subject. Some Cubans hoped that favorable trade treaties would boost their economy, yet many wanted to disengage themselves from any involvement with the United States, fearing that their powerful neighbor would take over complete control of the country.

After the war, most Cubans admitted that the government was unjust and corrupt. Batista and his cronies had assumed power as poor people and had finished as multimillionaires. In 1952 three men campaigned in the presidential election. On March 10, three months before the election was to take place, Batista led a bloodless revolt and took control of the country, declaring himself the supreme dictator.

Opposition to Batista's corruption grew among all classes of Cubans. The protests were led by university students, among them a young lawyer named Fidel Castro. Castro went to court to try to have the dictatorial government declared illegal, but he failed to bring about any concessions. The only alternative seemed to be force by the military.

JULY 26, 1953

On July 26, 1953, approximately 125 Cubans planned to attack a large army base at Moncada, near Santiago. Word of the surprise attack leaked to military officials. The rebels were either captured or killed. Among those captured was Fidel Castro. Standing before a judge, Castro made a fiery speech in his defense that lasted two hours. He denounced Batista, defended his own actions, and set forth a political program that included a return to a democratic rule under the 1940 constitution.

Although the speech was not heard by many, it was later published as *History Will Absolve Me*, a famous, often-quoted manifesto. Fidel Castro and his brother, Raúl Castro, were imprisoned on the Isle of Pines. They and others who had fought for independence became the heroes of the hour. Fi-

CUBA UNDER BATISTA

During Batista's second term in office, gambling, vice, and bribery were the rule. Organized crime gained a strong foothold in the tourist industry. Most of the visitors were more concerned with having a good time than with bothering to think about the harsh life the average Cuban faced.

In the early 1950s the *Saturday Evening Post* investigated the scene and said they could only find two honest places to gamble in Havana. One was under the grandstand of a race-track where locals would wager, and the other was the Mont-martyre casino, owned by Meyer Lansky, a convicted criminal from the underworld of the United States. In his book *Cuba from Conquistador to Castro*, Geoff Simons writes, "So curiously, the arrival of U.S. criminals meant more honest gambling. These professionals knew that you had to offer some chance of winning if you wanted to draw in the high roller."

Bribes were a common way of doing business, and many a cash gift was accepted by Batista himself. Before he was forced out of office, he had accumulated great wealth, which he took with him out of the country.

nally, under public pressure, Batista granted amnesty to all political prisoners. The prison gates were opened, but the rebels were banished from Cuba, forcing them to find asylum in other Latin American countries. In May 1955 Castro and his brother left for Mexico, but they had no intention of giving up.

Castro and his fellow revolutionaries trained in combat tactics, planning to return and overthrow Batista's government. Much had to be done. Funds had to be raised just to feed the men who were being trained. Ammunition had to be purchased. And most important, communication had to be maintained with revolutionary sympathizers within Cuba itself.

To defeat Batista, the fires of revolt would have to be kept burning. University students continued their demonstrations. The phrase "26th of July" continued to be painted on walls and fences. It was their rallying cry.

PLAN OF ATTACK

Castro was joined by a new patriot, who had been working for reform in his own country. His name was Ernesto "Che"

FIDEL CASTRO

Fidel Castro was born on August 13, 1926, on a farm in Oriente province (at the eastern end of Cuba). His family was moderately well-off, and he attended good Catholic schools in Santiago de Cuba and in Havana. He adjusted to the spartan regime of a Jesuit boarding school, Colegio de Belen.

He was a conscientious student, but his main ambition while still a teen was to play professional baseball. He was a good athlete, but not quite ready for the pro teams in the United States, where all young players hoped to find a spot. Instead, he continued with his academic studies and graduated in 1950 with a law degree from the University of Havana. Officially he has the title of Dr. Fidel Castro, but he never uses it.

Before graduation, Castro married Mirta Díaz-Balart in 1948. Their son, Fidel Castro Díaz-Balart, was born in 1949. Although Castro's marriage ended in a divorce in 1954, he has kept in close contact with his son, who has served as head of Cuba's atomic energy commission.

Castro, who has no rivals for power, lives a rather spartan life in comparison with the leaders who preceded him. He is most often seen wearing the fatigue uniform of the army without officer insignia. There is no mistaking his identity, though. He is an imposing figure, taller than those serving around him.

When he speaks to the public, he uses dramatic gestures and shouted prose. His speeches have been known to last two or three hours at a time and yet keep his audience's interest. In no small measure, the Cuban Revolution is Castro's revolution.

Cuba's longtime leader, Fidel Castro.

Guevara, and he was a twenty-seven-year-old doctor from Argentina.

Castro's planned invasion of Cuba by way of Mexico was set for November 30, 1956, three years after their first strike. The landing would occur on the coast near the city of Manzanillo. To distract the Cuban army, an uprising of local residents of Santiago was planned for the same day. The diversionary skirmishes took place right on schedule, but problems developed.

Castro and eighty-one companions crowded aboard the *Granma*, a private yacht designed to carry only fourteen passengers and crew. The time of the landing was delayed because of stormy weather and a faulty bilge pump. The boat was on the verge of sinking.

It was not until the morning of December 2 that the rebels finally set foot on Cuban soil. The landing was disastrous. The *Granma* went aground in shallow water, and it was impossible for the rebels to bring ashore any of their heavy equipment. All they could salvage was a gun apiece, with very little ammunition. Once ashore they were completely lost. They had expected to be met by a volunteer ground

Castro and his fellow rebels aboard the Granma. *Overloaded, the small boat ran aground during the invasion of Cuba.*

CHE GUEVARA

Ernesto "Che" Guevara is considered as close to a sainted hero as Castro will permit. If he had lived to offer competition, however, this might have been a different story.

He was born in Rosario, Argentina, on June 14, 1928, to parents with an aristocratic lineage who had lost most of their wealth. He was never a healthy young man, suffering from an asthmatic condition. He was a poet, without military training, but he could influence people with a charismatic harangue of words.

He had long black straggly hair and a beard, and he always dressed in army fatigues. The withering gaze of his intense eyes could connect with individuals so that they never forgot his message.

His life was one of rebellion, and he searched for causes. It was while Castro was training troops in Mexico that Guevara joined the revolutionary forces. He fought with the rebel forces when they were in hiding in the mountains. Castro later appointed Guevara to cabinet posts in the newly formed government. He became one of the most powerful leaders in framing the government of the people.

The Cuban Revolution would not hold his interest for long, though. He fought wherever he felt people were deprived of their rights. At one time he joined an army in the African Congo. Later he turned his energy to an uprising in Bolivia. It was here that he was captured and executed on October 9, 1967. When the news was received, Cuba went into mourning. Today tributes in statues, paintings, and posters are seen everywhere. Che Guevara is regarded as the spiritual leader of the Cuban Revolution.

The Argentinean-born revolutionary Che Guevara.

Batista (pictured) arrested and tortured more than twenty-five thousand people suspected of helping Castro and his small group of rebels.

force. Most members of this support group had been captured when word of the surprise attack was leaked to Batista's army. Castro's men gave up their planned attack on Manzanillo and began a march to the mountains.

HIDING OUT

Batista's army found the *Granma* and proof that Fidel Castro had been aboard. Now a price was put on his head. Batista sent his troops to search the area. Although they were not found, Batista announced to the press that most of the men had been killed in the act of barbarous treachery against their country.

It was a small band of rebels that huddled together in the highlands, but determination and the fiery words of their leader kept them bound together with vows that they would never surrender. Castro's men had lost all of their food.

They lived for many days on the juice of sugarcane, afraid to make contact with anyone for fear of capture. Eventually most of them reached Pico Turquino, the highest peak in the Sierra Maestra range. At this elevation they commanded a view of the surrounding territory with no chance for a surprise attack.

For Castro and his men, the first task was to survive and to win the confidence of the mountain peasants. Slowly the farmers in the region surrounding the peaks lost their distrust of the rebel soldiers with their tattered uniforms and bearded faces. Word spread to cities that the rebel army was still intact, and help was given.

HELP ON THE WAY

At first small sacks of food appeared at secret collection points. Then medical supplies and medical personnel came to their aid. For three years Castro and his men existed only through the assistance of the poorest people of Cuba. When medical care was available, Castro insisted that the peasants who had been helping them receive equal care.

While they were waiting for the right moment to regroup and attack, Che Guevara started a school for peasant children. So many children of all ages flocked to classes that soon another had to be opened. Helpful knowledge about better farming practices was also shared. Trust was growing, and sympathy for the cause of rebellion was spreading.

Still the rebels managed to elude the well-armed militia. Batista retaliated with a reign of terror. Anyone thought to have given aid to the rebels was arrested. In the final days of Batista's rule, the secret police tortured and killed more than twenty-five thousand people. In the meantime, Castro and his rebel forces destroyed sugar mills, burned crops, cut communication lines, and ambushed Batista's soldiers whenever possible.

Many innocent victims, who had not taken part in rebel activities, were put in prison. Those who survived were more than willing to join the forces that promised to bring about a humanitarian peace. The terror that Batista used to bring the people under his rule acted against him. Castro and his forces were immensely popular. The Cuban army itself was demoralized. They, too, could see that Batista's rule of terror had to end.

World opinion was on the side of the rebels. The United States was well aware that Cuba was turning into a police state, but it was afraid that conditions would worsen following a rebel victory. Instead of sending a military force to aid the rebels, President Dwight D. Eisenhower ordered an arms embargo on all trade with Cuba.

It was now time for action. Castro ordered his two top combat leaders, Camilo Cienfuegos and Che Guevara, to take rebel troops across the swamps and plains of the Camagüey province to cut the country in two. Many soldiers in the Cuban army laid down their arms without a fight. They wanted no part in yet another civil war. Their popular support went to the underdogs. Batista recognized that he was losing the battle.

VICTORY

On January 1, 1959, Batista boarded a plane for the Dominican Republic, leaving Cuba forever. Castro was not willing to accept a partial victory. He announced that the army and police of the cities must surrender. He also announced that criminals would stand trial. There would be no looting or killing of *chivatos*, or stool pigeons; they would eventually be brought to trial. Those trials sent many informers to prison immediately.

Fidel Castro's brother, Raúl, maintained order in Santiago while Fidel marched triumphantly into Havana.

On January 2 Castro took over Fort Moncada. He left his brother Raúl to keep order in Santiago. Then he began a triumphal trip down the length of the island to Havana. He waved to crowds from aboard a tank confiscated from the national military.

Fidel Castro, at the head of his romantic, ragged, and bearded rebel army, was now Cuba's leader, hero, and savior. For the poor rural peasants, he was their spokesman and their hope for the future.

5

Castro Has His Way

Even before his triumphant march through the nation's capital, Castro had been planning how to reorganize the government. He had little political experience himself, beyond being a charismatic military leader. Instead of taking on the number-one position himself, he chose another to become the first president of the new Cuba.

On January 1, 1959, Manuel Urrutia Lleo was sworn in as president. He was a respected judge who had earned a reputation for loyalty and honesty. He had stood up to Batista by challenging the army's murder of Fidel's small force after the 26th of July revolution. He had refused to punish rebels who had been captured after the ill-fated landing of the *Granma*. He left the country in exile, but he continued to raise money for the revolution. Early in December he had returned to Cuba with a planeload of armaments for the rebel army. Now that peace had come, Urrutia was the logical choice to lead the new government.

Not all Cubans shared the peasants' faith in this revolutionary government, but most were ready to give the new regime the chance to improve conditions. Probably at no other time in Cuban history was there such a feeling of exhilarating unity of purpose in the country. Castro and his followers became a kind of Robin Hood clan in the eyes of Cubans, taking property away from the wealthy and giving to the poor. There was much that needed to be changed.

Life as It Had Been
Before the Revolution

The exhilaration was short-lived. Cuba was in terrible financial shape. The average yearly income for a family of six was $590.75, and that included the value of whatever they grew and consumed themselves. Most of their diet was made up of rice, beans, and root vegetables. Only four people out of a hundred ate meat regularly.

After Batista's overthrow, Fidel Castro (pictured) chose Manuel Urrutia to become president. Leaving Urrutia in charge at home, Castro went abroad to drum up foreign support for the new Cuban government.

Most poor people had to pay for their own medical expenses when doctors were available. According to statistics published in 1958 by Cuba's Agrupación Católica University, more than a third of the people surveyed had intestinal parasites, 14 percent either had tuberculosis or had contracted it in the past, and 13 percent had contracted typhus.

These were not the only problems that faced the poor. Nine out of ten homes had no running water and depended on kerosene lamps for light. Fewer than half the houses had so much as an outdoor privy.

Too many people competed for too few jobs, and those with little education were seldom able to improve their living standards. Most of the peasants had never attended school and could neither read nor write. Of those who had some schooling, 88 percent had not gone beyond the third grade.

MORE PROBLEMS

The new government faced other daunting problems. Much of the land that should have been producing food was not being cultivated. Sugar had been the cash crop, but when prices went down, the land was left unplanted. Instead, $168 million worth of food was being imported every year, and the cost of shipping these items made them extremely expensive.

A typical family in Cuba before Castro came to power. With no running water and poor sanitation, many of the poor suffered from intestinal parasites, typhus, and tuberculosis.

Almost all hard goods, cars, farming machinery, and factory equipment was made in the United States. Eighty percent of utilities, such as telephones and electric power, was controlled by the United States. Ninety percent of the cattle ranches, 70 percent of the mines, nearly 100 percent of the oil refining industry, and 50 percent of the railway system were also U.S.-controlled. To top it off, 40 percent of the sugar industry, which accounted for most of the 1958 export earnings, was owned by U.S. businesses. Even when profits were realized in these fields, the benefits were all funneled to the owners and corporations in the United States.

Cubans resented that money earned from their labor and their land was flowing directly to the country that had been supplying Batista with tanks, guns, and military advisers. Batista and his cronies had grown rich and powerful with American help while the average Cuban struggled to feed his family.

This led to hard feelings between the countries from the very outset. Eisenhower did not trust the new rebel government, and Castro had no trust in the ally of his former enemy.

Although Cuba's new leaders did not want the United States to dictate their governing policies, they knew they needed financial help. Therefore, Castro did not publicly admit that he planned a communist form of government for Cuba because he knew the United States would oppose him.

With Castro's backing, the more moderate Manuel Urrutia Lleo was elected president of Cuba, with Castro as prime minister. Almost immediately conflict developed between the two leaders because of Urrutia's anticommunist feelings. Castro was initially unable to dismiss the new president because Urrutia was a patriot and was considered to be an honest man. Castro resigned his post on the governing council temporarily and waited to see what reforms would be put into place.

Conditions did not improve, and Urrutia's popularity could not equal the military-hero image of Castro held by the common voter. Urrutia was forced to resign. On July 18 still another president, Osvaldo Dorticos Torrado, was elected by the governing council and by popular vote. A loyal friend of Castro, Dorticos announced to a cheering crowd that Castro had agreed to resume his post as prime minister. Castro's first job was to cement friendly relations with the United States in return for financial aid.

DIPLOMATIC RELATIONS WITH THE UNITED STATES

Castro and an "advisory committee" of some seventy members of the military elite arrived in Washington, D.C., to discuss further trade relations with the United States. Financial aid was offered if Cuba would set up a democratic form of government. Castro immediately declined, saying he would not allow the United States to dictate policy to an independent foreign country.

Yet Castro appeared before the U.S. Foreign Relations Committee to assure his audience that American and other foreign interests would be fully protected in Cuba. He felt slighted that Eisenhower had not met with him personally. Instead, Eisenhower had decided on a game of golf in Atlanta, and a meeting with Vice President Richard Nixon was scheduled. Nixon later stated his view of the Cuban leader: "My first impression of him was that he was simply an idealistic and impractical young man."[7]

Castro's plans for Cuba were little changed by his visit to the United States. Both before and after the visit he was committed to social reforms, but not to establishing the democratic government desired by the United States. Castro did not think democracy would benefit his people. In Castro's own words, "real democracy is not possible for hungry people."[8]

From the beginning, Castro treated the Cuban people as his children, to be cared for and protected as long as they obeyed their father. He was sure he knew what was best for the country. A constitution would just hamper the revamping of the governmental system, Castro believed, so a constitution was never adopted. Instead, laws and regulations were written by representatives of Cuba's Popular Socialist

Fidel Castro (center) visits the United States to discuss trade relations and foreign aid. Castro's insistence on a Communist government for Cuba antagonized U.S. leaders.

Party. In the early days, such rules were "voted" into existence by popular acclamation at mass rallies.

STATE OWNERSHIP OF LANDS

The first stage of the Cuban Revolution was characterized by the liquidation of old power groups. The military, political parties, labor unions, and agricultural and professional associations were disbanded and replaced by new revolutionary bodies, such as the Rebel Army and the Comites de Defensiva de la Revolución.

The Agrarian Reform Law of May 1959 confiscated all property that had been owned by Batista and his supporters and turned it over to the people who had been working the land. The size of farms was limited so that there would be a share for all.

The final step was to put all sugar-growing lands in the hands of the government as well as to introduce the collectivization of all sugar mills. The running of the mills was handed over to the employees, with a short training period to give them instruction in the management of the business. The private families who had owned these assets could no longer hoard the profits for their personal use. There was an attempt to redistribute income from the wealthy classes to the lower- and middle-income sectors. Utility rates, taxes, and rents were reduced.

U.S. president Dwight D. Eisenhower decided to play golf rather than meet personally with Castro.

Over four hundred large Cuban-owned companies were also declared property of the state. Even small businesses, ranging from beauty parlors to hot dog stands, became government property. Almost every Cuban became a government employee, and all private and religious schools were turned into state institutions. Likewise, all newspapers, magazines, and radio and television programming was managed by the government. No avenue for debate existed. On the radio, Castro's voice was heard in long tirades against any opposition. Castro retained popular support despite these restrictive measures because many Cubans were dissatisfied with the Batista government that had strangled much of Cuban life with corruption and crime for most of the previous three decades.

COMMUNISM TAKES OVER

Disregarding statements made to his American hosts during his visit to Washington, Castro's government took control of all U.S. enterprises within Cuba, even the banking institutions. The total worth of seized U.S. property was estimated at $2 billion. In retaliation, President Eisenhower broke off all diplomatic relations with Cuba in January 1961. The U.S. government canceled all purchases of Cuban sugar, and shortly thereafter imposed a complete embargo against all trade with Cuba, a condition that still exists today.

The Cuban government had kept its promise to the underprivileged masses that had backed the rebellion. In doing so, it had made enemies of the traditional property-owning classes. It was at this time that many former landowners packed up and immigrated to Florida, waiting for the time when they expected Castro would be thrown out of power. Opposition outside the country was also growing, and Cubans in the United States were organizing their efforts.

COUNTERREVOLUTION

The counterrevolution did not begin suddenly or dramatically. Through all the broken pledges of free elections and free press, Castro remained the unchallenged leader. He was still *El Caballo* ("The Horse"), the romantic legendary liberator from the hills. But for Cuban exiles, who had lost all that they had owned in their native country, another war for freedom seemed imminent. Cuban exiles began operating in Guatemala under U.S. direction in the spring of 1960.

Aware that there could be danger from outside the country, Castro used fiery words to keep the loyalty of those who had been pulled from poverty to moderate affluence. The United States was pictured as the villain, wanting to keep the wealth of Cuba for itself. Now it was time for Cubans to show their support for the regime that had enhanced their future. Cubans were urged to celebrate their loyalty by volunteering their time to defend their country. They were ordered to be loyal to their government and to work for a brighter future for themselves and their children. The young and old alike spent time after school and work training with the militia to defend their country against attack.

BAY OF PIGS

Castro was right. The attack was about to begin. Early on the morning of April 15, 1961, eight B-26 bombers flew over Cuba with bombs, rockets, and machine-gun fire, aiming their missiles at three military airfields. All eight bombers bore the markings of the Cuban air force so as not to attract attention before their bombs were dropped. In the event that they were forced down, they had been instructed to say that they were pilots of the Cuban air force who had defected. But in reality, they were Cuban exiles who had been trained by Americans in Guatemala and Nicaragua.

The exile force was made up of a fourteen-hundred-man army that was to fight its way ashore, a fleet of seven ships to carry the men from Nicaragua to Cuba, and an air force of B-26 bombers and six cargo planes. Sixty-one Cuban pilots, navigators, and radio operators manned the exiles' air force.

At dawn on April 17 the bombers began to fly in pairs over the beaches of the Bay of Pigs to provide cover for the ground troops. They expected no opposition, thinking that the earlier raids on Cuban military airfields had destroyed all of Castro's air defense. Instead, they discovered that the air force had enough fighter planes to destroy the rebel bombers, which lacked defenses. Their guns had been removed to increase their range and bomb load.

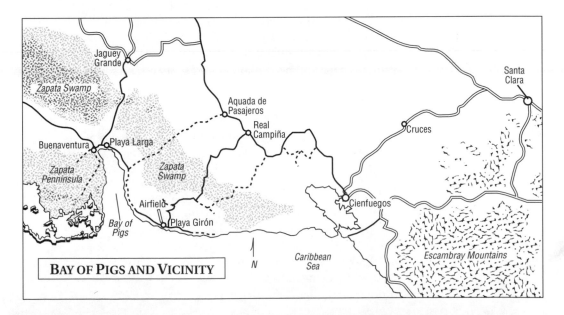

BAY OF PIGS AND VICINITY

The rebels who had landed by sea, however, secured a beachhead against light opposition. They had expected to be greeted enthusiastically by farmers in the area. After all, they had come to save Cuba from the terrorism of a dictator. The expected support did not materialize. Sympathy was easily mustered for those killed in the air raids that had preceded the landing. Despite a barrage of radio broadcasts originating in the United States that urged Cubans to revolt and to sabotage the local government, they remained staunchly loyal to Castro. Most of the invaders were killed. Castro's militia rounded up the remaining scattered exile survivors, who received life sentences in Cuban prisons.

In Washington, D.C., President John F. Kennedy decided not to order the marines to save the defeated rebel troops. The U.S. government repeatedly denied any knowledge of the exiles' plan to invade Cuba. Though the exile force was nominally under the direction of the Cuban Revolutionary

THE BAY OF PIGS

Castro spoke despairingly of the brigade that landed at the Bay of Pigs, calling them war criminals and sons of the jaded rich who were coming to regain their vast holdings at the expense of the workers. In reality, Brigade 2506, its code name, was a cross section of Cuba. The men ranged in age from sixteen to sixty-one, with the average age being twenty-nine. There were peasants and fishermen as well as doctors, lawyers, and bankers. A large percentage of the men were married and had children, and there were a number of father-and-son pairs aboard the ships.

By profession, the 240 students were the largest group, but there were mechanics, teachers, artists, draftsmen, newspaper reporters, engineers, musicians, three Catholic priests, one Protestant minister, geologists, cattlemen, and clerks. With the exception of the 135 former professional soldiers, who had served under both Batista and Castro, most of the men had no previous military training or experience. Some had never even held a weapon until that weekend aboard ship.

Their motives varied. Some were stirred by hate, some by greed, some by adventure, but most, especially the young, felt a sense of duty and idealism.

It was a losing battle.

Council, a coalition of exile groups, they had been trained and funded by the U.S. government. Those involved hoped that Castro himself would be the captive and that a communist government would be defeated.

LINKS WITH RUSSIA

Instead, Castro's victory at the Bay of Pigs was a boost for his worldwide prestige and a blow to America's bungling attempt to bully a small nation into submission. Castro's position was stronger than ever, and he was now able to announce that a new Party of the Socialist Revolution was to be formed along the lines of Marxist and Leninist communism. Cuba now aligned itself officially with Soviet Russia and its satellite countries.

Experts from Czechoslovakia were brought to Cuba to help plan the island's economy. Everything needed to industrialize the nation had to be purchased abroad. Cuba was short on cash and even short on food. Inadequate distribution of food caused some of the problems. Also weather conditions could wipe out the cash crop of sugar when either a drought, like the one that occurred in 1962, or a wild hurricane, like the ones that swept through in 1963, caused damage. Reliance on sugar could not insure monetary stability.

After the Bay of Pigs, Castro became even more enamored of the Communist system originally advocated by Karl Marx (pictured).

In the spring of 1962 the Cuban government had to impose food rationing. Again the United States was sure that the Cuban people would disapprove and throw out the dictator. That did not happen. The Organization of American States (OAS), however, which represents other Latin American countries, was afraid that Castro's communism threatened governments and formally excluded Cuba from the organization in February 1962. All Latin American countries except Mexico broke off relations with Cuba, leaving the nation with only one important partner, the USSR.

THE MISSILE CRISIS

The United States and the Soviet Union were in the middle of what was a long and bitter struggle referred to as the Cold War. Both were vying for world domination. Cuba had won

ERECTOR ON LAUNCH PAD

MISSILE READY BLDGS

OXIDIZER VEHICLES

PROB HYDROGEN PEROXIDE TANKS

MISSILE READY BLDGS

FUELING VEHICLES

TENTS

ERECTOR ON LAUNCH PAD

MISSILE ON TRAILER

A U.S. reconnaissance photo reveals the location of a Cuban missile base.

Soviet support by defying its northern neighbor. The USSR now saw an opportunity to strengthen Cuba's defensive position. It would give the Soviet nation a military base close to its enemy. Cuba was being armed with nuclear warheads.

The secret was soon discovered. U.S. planes with sensitive infrared cameras were able to detect the new installations. They could also tell that airfield landing strips were being expanded and jet bombers, capable of carrying out nuclear bombing raids against the United States, were being delivered to Cuba.

On October 22, 1962, President Kennedy explained these frightening facts on a nationwide television broadcast. Kennedy decided to take immediate steps to halt the buildup of war matériel. He called on Nikita Khrushchev of the Soviet Union to either dismantle all missile launch sites and remove all military equipment or to expect a missile attack from the United States on Cuba.

In speaking to the American public, Kennedy said, "I call upon him further to abandon this course of world domination. . . . Our goal is not the victory of might, but the vindication of right—not peace at the expense of freedom, but both peace and freedom, here in this hemisphere, and, we hope, around the world." [9]

The OAS supported the actions of the United States and endorsed the use of force against Cuba. U.S. warships steamed toward the waters off the Cuban coast to enforce a blockade so that no shipping of any sort could leave or enter its ports.

Twenty-five ships from socialist countries were reported heading for Cuban waters, where the U.S. Navy waited to intercept them. Khrushchev said that any interference with Soviet shipping on the high seas would be an act of war. The world waited anxiously, expecting that a third world war was imminent.

President Kennedy addresses the nation, informing the American public of the presence of Soviet nuclear missiles in Cuba.

A U.S. destroyer (top) intercepts a tanker bound for Cuba as part of the American naval blockade.

Only through negotiation by the United Nations was war averted. The Soviet Union agreed to suspend shipments of arms, the United States volunteered to suspend the blockade, and Cuba agreed to suspend construction of military installations while negotiations were held. Finally, the world was able to breathe easier again.

BACKING DOWN

The missile crisis had far-reaching effects. China maintained that Premier Khrushchev had backed down way too easily. And Castro was disillusioned by the Soviet Union's agreement to settle without consulting the Cuban government. Castro had been anxious to have the United States agree to withdraw its forces from Guantánamo. The naval base had always been a thorn in the side of Cuba since the independent nation believed no foreign nation should have the right to have a military base on its soil.

However, there was little that Castro could do. He had tried to turn the country into a self-sufficient, industrialized nation, but he had failed through poor planning and a lack of trained personnel and resources. He needed Soviet help.

In 1970 he rallied the country to beat their record of sugarcane tonnage for export to pay for other needed goods.

Office workers, soldiers, and even schoolchildren were recruited as volunteers in the field. The goal was not met, and the economy actually worsened because workers were taken from their regular jobs.

In 1972 Cuba joined the Council for Mutual Assistance, an organization established to coordinate the affairs of all Soviet-bloc countries. Although Castro violently refuted the claim that Cuba had become a flunky only doing the bidding of the Soviet Union, it was obvious that her ties were being drawn closer and closer to the communist superpower.

In 1976 the Cuban government finally adopted a new constitution modeled on Soviet principles. Around this time, Cuba also began to send its troops, well armed with Soviet weapons, to other parts of the world trying to set up communist governments. Cubans fought alongside Marxist forces in the African countries of Angola, Ethiopia, and Mozambique. They were flown in Soviet planes to back revolutionary armies in Central and South America and in the Middle East.

THE BOAT PEOPLE

Protests and outcries from Cubans who were suffering hard times in their own country were becoming more and more vocal, and many were arrested. Finally, in March 1980 about

CASTRO'S FIVE-POINT PROGRAM

During negotiations to end the missile crisis, Castro presented five demands in exchange for the dismantling of the missile sites. They are listed in Stephen Williams's book *Cuba: The Land, the History, the People, the Culture.*

1. An end to the economic embargo and all commercial pressures.

2. An end to all subversive activities by the United States against Cuba.

3. An end to "pirate attacks" from bases in the United States and Puerto Rico.

4. An end to violations of Cuban air and naval space.

5. A United States withdrawal from the Guantánamo naval base.

No written agreement was ever made to address these points of contention.

eleven thousand protesting citizens stormed the Peruvian embassy in Havana seeking political asylum. They begged for a way to leave the country. U.S. president Jimmy Carter approved an order permitting immigration. Castro declared the port of Mariel open to anyone who wanted to leave. He was surprised and embarrassed by the numbers who came forward to accept the offer.

It occurred to Castro that this was a way to get rid of many of his own undesirables. Prisons were emptied of dangerous criminals and hospitals discharged of some of their sickest patients.

A difficult decision had to be made. Would the United States turn away relatives of exiled Cubans who had been waiting to embrace their families, or would it take the bad along with the good? For humane reasons, President Carter chose the latter course. Between April and September 1980, over 125,000 Cubans fled their country. Thousands more were waiting to do so. Castro finally had to put a stop to the exodus, but when transportation was cut off, families resorted to any type of boat or raft that could take them to the United States. Many perished at sea.

POLITICAL CHANGES IN THE USSR

Now that so many dissatisfied Cubans had left the country, Castro was hoping for little opposition in running the country the way he saw fit. He still had to find a way to balance the

TROOPS TO GRENADA

Following Castro's foreign policy of fighting for rebel causes to promote communist governments elsewhere, Castro sent an army to the small Caribbean island of Grenada in October 1983. The bloody confrontation resulted in the killing of several of Grenada's top government officials.

The Organization of Eastern Caribbean States formally asked U.S. president Ronald Reagan to intervene, fearful that their own countries would be invaded by Cubans. U.S. Marines were sent to gain a peaceful settlement.

Marines overpowered the army of Grenada and the Cuban officers who had led them. As a result, some one thousand Cubans were expelled from Grenada.

Soviet president Mikhail Gorbachev announced the cutoff of aid to Cuba as a result of the Soviet Union's economic problems.

debts that Cuba was accumulating, but suddenly the open policy with the Soviet Union was being withdrawn.

In March 1985 Mikhail Gorbachev was elected the new head of the Soviet Union. The USSR, too, was having severe economic problems. By 1990 Cuba had the largest debt to the USSR of all socialist countries. Government officials announced that no more financial help would be forthcoming.

Gorbachev was about to try a new political tack, *glasnost* (openness) and *perestroika* (restructuring). It meant that USSR and Eastern Europe were set on a course to encourage a free economy and multiparty political systems. Castro denounced the new programs as madness.

He vowed to be the world leader to continue the ideals of communism and maintain reverence for its founders. He said, "When others are . . . removing Lenin's name from streets and parks and destroying statues of Marx, Lenin, and Engels, we will continue to build them here." [10]

Castro's Communist regime holds fast despite the economic collapse of other Communist nations.

By the 1990s Cuba had become the only country left in the world, with the possible exception of North Korea, with a Soviet-style Communist regime. Castro rejected all market-oriented reforms, further restraining private ownership even in what had been free peasant markets. He integrated more private farms into state-controlled cooperatives, eliminating small private manufacturers, truckers, and street vendors. He also restricted private construction and the selling or renting of much-needed housing. Castro ends all of his speeches with the slogan, Socialism or Death.

Without access to Soviet help, Castro limited imports and reduced rationed quotas of food. Wages were cut, reemphasizing unpaid voluntary labor. Cuba was facing a crisis, although Castro refused to admit it in his speeches.

THE CULTURE OF CUBA

Before Castro's rise to power, the overwhelming majority of Cubans identified themselves as Roman Catholics. In 1961 the rebel government banned all religious processions and abolished religious holidays. Many dissenters were sentenced to labor camps. Only a few older residents, who had been brought up in the faith, had the courage and the determination to worship in private.

Many devout exiles tried to keep the faith alive by writing to those who were left behind. News of the visit of Pope John Paul II to Cuba in 1998 was a surprise to many and was met with great anticipation. As one construction worker says, "We'd always been told that the Church was on the wrong side of the revolution." [11] Revolutionary sentiment maintained that the church did little to help the poor before Castro came to power, so it was up to the government to see to the people's needs.

CASTRO AND THE POPE

For five days in February 1998 Cubans and the world, by way of radio and television, heard the pope's words and saw the crowds surrounding him. It seemed strange to see old warriors, who had spent much of their careers openly fighting each other's faith, sharing a platform and exchanging words. For Castro, it was the time to be in the world spotlight as the benevolent savior of the poor instead of as the violent dictator that his enemies portrayed.

Castro refrained from wearing army fatigues, which is his usual attire. Instead, he wore a navy blue suit and an unaccustomed smile. Yet his words still brought a sting. He denounced the United States as trying to commit "genocide" against the Cuban people with the embargo that denied Cubans food and medicine. He stressed that he and the pope shared a concern about the excesses of capitalism. Moreover, if anybody had ideas about changing communism in Cuba,

69

Pope John Paul II and Fidel Castro chat during the pope's five-day visit to Cuba in 1998. Cuba was once a devoutly Catholic country, but Catholicism was firmly rejected by Castro's government.

Castro was quick to say, "We would choose a thousand times death rather than renounce our convictions." [12]

The pope refrained from entering the argument, but he criticized what had happened in Cuba without a strong religious platform. He called abortion, which takes place in Cuba at a rate of sixty for every one hundred live births, an abominable crime, and he said that parents should have the freedom to choose their children's religion. These words were greeted with applause.

At this time, no one can guess what long-reaching effects the pope's visit will have on the religious commitment of the people. As Father Raúl Núñez says, "There is no religious culture here. We are starting at zero." [13]

Although it was not unusual to hear new churchgoers call the pope "comrade" instead of "Your Holiness," it was the first time in forty years that even a hint of acceptance of worship was uttered.

SANTERIA

A small percentage of the Cuban people still practice a secretive religion brought over from Africa by slaves. Santeria, sometimes called Lucimi, combines the worship of African gods and those deified by the Catholic Church. Saint Barbara, for instance, is seen as the incarnation of Chango, the African deity of fire, lightning, and thunder. Certain high priests and priestesses are thought to have the power to create magic spells, both for the good of one's health and for the punishment of one's enemies.

Followers of Santeria believe that a person's destiny is determined before birth and that a heavenly universe exists that is ruled over by Olifi, who is so spiritual that humans cannot hope to communicate directly with him. Only through the priests of this religion, whose powers are frequently passed on from one generation to another in a single family, can the will of Olifi be interpreted to the rest of the human race. The word "*Santeria*" literally means "saint worship."

Santeria appeals to many people because it does not have the strict moral sanctions that Catholicism does; instead it helps to excuse wrongdoings. It is a very private and mysterious faith, the power of which rests in its magical nature. It has been almost impossible to outlaw people from practicing Santeria rituals because they are usually performed in the middle of the night in some rural area.

HOLIDAYS

The one holiday permitted that blends both Catholic and African rites is Cuba's annual Carnival. It is much like the Mardi Gras of New Orleans, with people dressed in fantastic

BLACK VIRGINS

Few works of art bear the stamp of Cuban concepts so completely as the number of black Virgins that have been painted and sculpted over the years. A well-known example is the Virgin of Regia, Havana's spiritual patron, worshipped in a colonial church near the bay of Havana.

She is clothed in blue fabric with silver embroidery. Her skin is black, but she holds a lily-white child, expressing the popular ethnic belief that black Africa produced the origin of the human race.

In other countries the Virgin Mary and others almost always appear as white women with features resembling what European artists of the fifteenth, sixteenth, and seventeenth centuries thought were most appealing. These Cuban artists feature the beauty of black icons.

costumes as they dance in the streets. Its real origin was as a celebration for the end of the sugar harvest. Slaves had time off from work, and it was a time of rejoicing.

By tradition it was held in late July, the date varying with the bounty of the harvest, but Castro has made it a celebration to commemorate the beginning of the rebellion he led on July 26, 1953. Cuba's Carnival is now considered the official celebration of national independence.

Hundreds of thousands of Cubans crowd Havana's Plaza de Revolución in celebration of Communism and workers' rights on May Day in 1996.

January 1 is not celebrated as New Year's Day, but instead as Day of Liberation in observance of President Batista's flight from office and the country. The government also recognizes the second Monday in October as War of Independence Day after the war fought in 1868.

As in many communist countries, May 1 is International Workers' Day. Floats decorated by various industrial groups and farmworkers are led in street parades by military troops, and children in school uniforms march with their parents.

MUSIC

Celebrating any holiday in Cuba requires music. Few countries have such a distinctive musical heritage as Cuba. Combining Spanish guitar and African drum, a special beat has melded into popular, jazz, and tribal compositions. During the early part of the twentieth century, Havana was noted for lavish nightclubs, dance halls, and gambling casinos that featured this type of music.

The small island has had as much influence on twentieth-century popular music as any country in the world. The conga, the rumba, the mambo, and the cha-cha were all inspired by Cuban musical numbers. World-renowned bandleaders include Xavier Cugat, Arturo "Chico" O'Farill, and Desi Arnez, and today Gloria Estefan and her band, the Miami Sound Machine, owe their success to the rhythms of Cuban music.

As long ago as 1875, France's Georges Bizet was influenced by Afro-Cuban rhythm as he wrote "Habanera" for his opera *Carmen*. That influence affected George Gershwin when he composed a Cuban overture using percussion instruments native to Cuba: the bongo drums; maracas, a kind of rattle; claves, or rhythm sticks; and the guiro, a notched gourd that produces a rasping sound when scraped.

Dancing is part of the soul of Cuba. Nearly every celebration, public or private, includes dancing. The most famous classical style is called the zapateo. Even the costumes follow

Gloria Estefan and the Miami Sound Machine are well known for incorporating Cuban musical rhythms into their compositions. Cuban music is a mixture of Latin, African, and Caribbean musical traditions.

tradition. The man wears white trousers, a pleated white shirt, a triangular red scarf around his neck, and a straw hat on his head. The woman wears the *bata criolla*, a long dress with flounces, usually white with red polka dots. It is shorter in the front and has a sort of train in the back. Its design is taken from the flamenco dancers of Spain.

Cubans also admire classical ballet. The Alicia Alonso National School of Ballet was created to train young dancers. The school is fully subsidized by the state, and there is a waiting list for hopeful young students.

Gonzalo Roig founded the Havana Symphony Orchestra. In 1932 he adapted the Cuban writer Cirilo Villaverde's work for an opera about love between a mixed-blood woman and a Spanish aristocrat. It was the first time that Cuban rhythms, such as the rumba and conga, had been combined with more classic styles.

THEATER AND FILM

During colonial times theater was one of the few recreational activities open to all social classes. The wealthy sponsored these plays, frequently given on stages that were available for everyone to view. Today Cuba has a strong theatrical movement, but many of the themes of the dramas follow a political line.

The Teatro Nacional in Havana is a spectacular example of a theater built during the golden age of architecture. In Cuba this era occurred during the later part of the nineteenth century, when wealthy landowners were trying to compete with European extravagances. The theater was built with columns, turrets, and elaborate interior murals. Today original plays written by Cubans and performed by talented local actors are given on a regular schedule.

The Institute of Cinematographic Art and Industry was created to give Cuba a chance to compete in the world market of filmmaking. Several films made in Cuba and directed by Cubans have received international awards. Also, an annual film festival is hosted in Havana, which has helped bring in tourists.

LITERATURE

Writers are often invited to Cuba in hopes that they may come away with good things to say about the beautiful island, and visitors are reminded of the long literary tradition in Cuba. As early as the 1700s writers began to publish literature describing their lives and times. Gertrudis Gómez de Avellaneda wrote novels condemning slavery, and the countess of Merlin described her world travels. Cirilo Villaverde is considered the major Cuban novelist of the nineteenth century. He frequently wrote about the wide discrepancy between social classes, but there was no moral lecturing for a change.

Cubans have always loved poetry. José Martí, known as the founder of the Cuban independence movement, was best recognized for his lyrical verse. Every Cuban child has been called on to memorize some of his work.

American Ernest Hemingway lived in Cuba for twenty years and won the Nobel Prize in literature. His books include one about a Cuban fisherman, *The Old Man and the Sea*. His home in Havana is now open to the public as a museum.

ART IN CUBA

Many fine museums are established in Cuba. On March 3, 1998, the sixth Havana Biennial Art Show brought many tourists to the capital city. The show opened with one of the largest displays of visual arts in the Western Hemisphere. Some 177 artists from 45 nations, mainly in Latin America, Africa, and Asia, were invited to submit their work. France, Great Britain, Japan, Australia, and the United States were represented by one artist each.

Cuban revolutionary José Martí is also well remembered as a writer.

Nineteen buildings were required to house the exhibits. The theme was "Memories," and many exhibitors chose collections of various items to tell their story.

Lidzie Alviza and Lázaro Savedra are two young Cubans who received world attention with their combination of wood sculpture and photography.

There were also some strange compositions, such as the clear plastic tubing that ran from one room to another. It was filled with pig blood, symbolically meaning that the fluid of life keeps people of all colors and ethnic backgrounds together as one human race.

In the past Cuban artists tended to follow European trends in art. Wealthy landowners of Spanish ancestry often wanted elaborate portraits to hang on their walls. Perhaps the best-known artist to follow this tradition was the Cuban-born black artist Vicente Escobar (1775–1834). Later, Esteban Chartrand (1840–1883) painted stylized romantic tropical landscapes that were popular.

Cuba's best-known sculptor, Juana José Sicre, died nine years after the revolution in 1968. She was one of the few women to exhibit internationally. Her works in stone and clay are displayed in Havana and also in Paris and in Buenos Aires. Wilfredo Lam's (1902–1983) surrealistic style combines both African and Cuban symbols.

With Castro's blessing, posters have become a prime vehicle for communicating with the masses, and patriotic themes are often used. Posters advertising the country's national sport of baseball deserve a place in an art gallery; they are well executed and are often collected as artwork.

SPORTS

Sports Illustrated magazine recently published an article entitled "The Best Little Sports Machine in the World." Without funding to pay Cuban athletes for their training time, have nevertheless set many sports records. At the Pan American Games in 1995 in Argentina, Cuba won 238 medals, more than any country except the United States. In the Summer Olympics, Cuba won the most medals per capita. Records show that Cuba has the world's best high jumper, best national volleyball players, best national baseball team, and best amateur boxers.

Manitoba, Canada, will host the 1999 Pan American Games, in which 42 countries will be competing in 34 different events. Cubans are already anticipating victories.

Cuba fell in love with the game of baseball at about the turn of the century and has been carrying on the tradition. Every small town has a team. Since Castro revolutionized the country there have been no professional sports, but there are still heroes of the game. Victor Mesa surpassed the all-time world record of 2,215 earned runs in 1996. The Cuban government pays him 318 pesos a month (about $8) while top players in the United States often earn six-figure salaries.

BÉISBOL

Despite trying to be independent from all forms of influence from the United States, Cuba considers baseball to be its national sport. One theory is that the game did not originate in the States but actually grew out of a game the Taino Indians played called *batey*. No matter where it started, Cubans have been wildly excited about baseball since the mid–nineteenth century. An engraving from this early time period shows a player standing at a base with a bat over his shoulder.

Stadiums in the cities have been built, but the real excitement of the game starts in the streets or the fields, wherever there are kids swinging bats made from broomsticks or shovel handles.

COMPETING ABROAD

Five Cubans played baseball in Japan in 1994. That number has increased, and others have since been sent to Italy. The government keeps 70 percent of the athletes' pay, and the state ensures their return by making them travel without their families—although many have sought political asylum despite this fact.

Ramon Ledon, a former member of the Cuban national boxing team, headed off on a raft for the Florida shore. He was picked up by a U.S. Coast Guard cutter and returned to the Guantánamo base, where he still waits for permission to legally enter the United States.

SPORTS AT HOME

Soccer and rugby are played on many school fields, but baseball is by far the most popular sport. Boxing comes in second. Cubans have won many international championships, but doing so takes intensive training. Few athletes have the resources to devote all their time to the preparation for world-class bouts.

Track-and-field events have given Cuba Olympic medals. Water sports are also popular because there is almost a year-round opportunity to compete in swimming, diving, rowing, and sailing events. Competitive cycling is a new organized sport in Cuba. And indoor pursuits such as chess and dominoes are very popular.

Members of the Cuban Olympic baseball team carry their flag in victory after defeating Japan in the 1996 Olympics. Baseball is the most popular sport in Cuba.

Cockfighting has been banned in some countries because of its cruelty to the birds, but in Cuba, with a long line of Spanish tradition, certain types of cocks are bred for fighting. Each cock has its own trainer, and the competition takes place in a small fenced circle called the *valla*. Sometimes sharp metal spurs are attached to the birds' legs. The fight continues until either one of the cocks is killed or "chickens out" by flying over the *valla*. A great deal of gambling takes place at such events.

NEWSPAPERS

Sporting events are covered in the local papers, but Cuban newspapers are getting thinner and thinner. *Granma*, named after the boat Castro and his rebel forces used in their original landing to take over Batista's army, is the national paper. It no longer is a daily and now has only four pages. Its international coverage has always been skimpy.

Castro has complete control over the information media. He has placed the idea in Cubans' minds that the United States is a current military threat. No amount of coaxing from foreign TV commentators or diplomats can alter Cubans' fear of invasion by foreign troops.

Castro is trying to improve the image his country has in overseas press releases. Recently a group of journalists from the United States was given access to the country for a brief conference with other writers. Cubans were vocal in giving their feelings about what they called "negative propaganda" about Cuban communist policies.

Many Cubans do not trust what is being said about them in other countries. One woman asked a U.S. journalist at the conference, "Will you print the truth, or will it be lies that are given to you by the *gusanos* (worms) who fled the country? They are puppets of the United States. They want to take Cuba back to capitalism. We are against the U.S. government." [14]

In comparing Cuba to other communist countries that are today going through reforms, one man said,

> Our land belongs to us. Cuba is not like Czechoslovakia or Hungary. We are 35 years building socialism and a new society for our children. . . . We are Caribbean, Spanish, African. We are absolutely different. This is the real Cuban people, not those across the water [meaning the Miami-based exiles]. [15]

Like other nations, modern Cuba has been molded by its leaders and its history. Cuban art, literature, music, and other elements of the nation's culture reflect the complex mix of events that have occurred over many centuries.

7

CUBA TODAY

Over half the population of Cuba today was born after the 1959 revolution. They have no way of comparing what life was like before that time. Was it better or worse? The answer is a little of both.

One of Castro's most impressive accomplishments is the rise of the literacy rate. Ninety-six percent of all Cubans can read and write. When he took over the government, that figure was only about 5 percent.

Castro accomplished this in one bold plan, which started in April 1961. Secondary schools and colleges were closed for one year so that groups of literate students could go into rural areas under the supervision of trained teachers to live with peasants and teach them how to read and write. During that year one generation of young people was denied a formal education, but hundreds of others were given the opportunity to further their learning.

SCHOOLING

All education is free, even at the university level. Preschool classes begin at age two, and children must attend school until they are fourteen. Castro has said that, with additional schools in the planning stage, he hopes to increase compulsory education through high school.

Many high schools are built around dormitory complexes where boys and girls live on campus. Most schools include a sports arena, dining hall, medical center, student store, and even a movie theater, as well as classrooms.

Food is provided and also clothing. Students wear uniforms issued by the government. These government schools also include working farms. School days start at six in the morning. Following breakfast, half the students go to their classes while the rest go to work on the farm. At the lunch break, the two groups change activities. The crops produced by the student body pay for the school's expenses.

Each day's schedule includes sports and frequently a program to encourage cultural pride in the arts. Plays and musical performances often mimic the political speeches aired on the local radio, but they do give students a much broader experience than they would have had without such a program.

Students are allowed about half an hour of free time before study hall and lights out. After morning classes on Saturday, students board buses to take them back to their homes, where they spend the night and return to school the next evening.

Children dressed in school uniforms read under the watchful gaze of Lenin's portrait. Cuba boasts a phenomenal literacy rate of 96 percent.

REQUIRED SUBJECTS

Required subjects include mathematics, physics, biology, geography, history, and the study of literature in both Spanish and English. There are also technical subjects to prepare students for specific jobs. One technical school gives students hands-on experience in assembling radios and televisions, and maintenance skills in working with automobiles and farm machinery. Although more than half of Cuba's population live in urban areas, agricultural work is also promoted.

Students must pass a strict code of examinations to be prepared for the next grade. Students with the best records are selected to go on to higher education. Some are chosen to prepare for jobs in teaching younger children, and they may even take on this job before their own graduation. The brightest students are sent on to one of Cuba's four universities, where degrees in engineering, medicine, economics, and social studies are offered.

ADULT EDUCATION

Adults are also encouraged to attend school. Each year over forty thousand adults sign up for free classes. Pride is fostered, and medals are awarded for accomplishments. Family events are planned around activities that are meant to enrich the social life of communities.

Cuba today has a higher standard of literacy than any other Third World country. This has all been accomplished in the last forty years.

HEALTH AND WELFARE

Another important step forward in helping the working-class Cuban family has been in the field of health care. This is the responsibility of the state's Ministry of Public Health. Only 53 out of 20,545 Cuban physicians were reported to have private practices in 1990. The rest work for and are paid by the government.

A large network of urban and rural hospitals and clinics has been established in all 14 provinces. According to available figures, Cuba has the best health record of any of the Latin American countries. Life expectancy today is 70 years compared to 48 in Bolivia. Malaria, diphtheria, whooping cough, polio, and measles have almost been wiped out. That is an amazing record considering that in the 1960s more than 3,000 physicians left Cuba.

The Ministry of Public Health reported that it was operating a total of 2,273 hospitals, which included 92 general hospitals, 21 maternity hospitals, 29 maternal-infant hospitals, and 27 pediatric hospitals. There are 85 homes for expectant mothers, 143 dental clinics, 65 homes for the elderly, and 14 homes for the disabled. Cuba's infant mortality rate is among the lowest in the world, a direct result of offering prenatal care for pregnant mothers.

PIONEERS

Most young people between the ages of seven and fourteen belong to the Organización de Pioneros José Martí, the Pioneers. This organization is similar in some ways to American scouting organizations, Future Farmers of America, and the YMCA and YWCA. Members of this group wear red berets and blue-and-white scarves with their school uniforms to set them apart.

Pioneers participate in community service, sports, and programs fostering music, art, or dance. There are also organizations for older university students. They participate in military drills to become patriotic members of the Communist Party. They are being trained to defend their country, especially against the possibility of foreign invasion.

Cuba's treatment of mental patients is a model for other nations. Havana Psychiatric Hospital patients are given work gardening, preparing food, cleaning, making uniforms and furniture, and entertaining patients with skits and musical performances. Too often in other countries, patients are kept isolated in hospital wards with nothing to occupy their minds.

The government is trying to reduce the incidence of all disease by improving the nation's hygiene, but one serious problem still exists. Since Russia has stopped its support of Cuba, and with the U.S. embargo on all goods, the supply of medical equipment and medicines has been dangerously low.

The United States has not lifted the ban on trading with Cuba, but since Pope John Paul II's visit to Cuba in 1998, a reconciliatory atmosphere has led to humanitarian relief. President Bill Clinton's revised terms make it easier for U.S. pharmaceutical and medical equipment companies to sell their products to Cuba. Clinton also announced that he will allow Cubans in the United States to send $300 every three months to relatives on the island. A United Nations report estimates that Cuba receives $800 million each year in much smaller unrecorded remittances. That amount surpasses Cuba's net income from sugar and tourism. Permitting an increase in this cash flow represents a sweeping political shift from 1996, when the long-standing U.S. trade embargo was tightened to punish Castro for shooting down two planes piloted by an exile group. It also represents a huge help to those cash-strapped Cubans who are lucky enough to have relatives in the United States.

These exiled relatives might be surprised at the changes that have been occurring in Cuba. Large landowners, who once ruled the lives of the poorly paid farmworkers, lost

LANGUAGE

In its written form, the language educated Cubans use is much the same as standard Spanish, but colloquial Spanish in Cuba differs from the language of Spain and from many other Latin American countries. It closely resembles the speech of Costa Rica, where some of the meaning and dialect of African words blend with conversation. Many Cubans feel a sense of pride that they have not lost a part of their heritage.

Cubans at work in a sugarcane factory. Though unemployment is almost nonexistent, few Cubans have the freedom to choose their careers.

much of their land to the government after the revolution. The smaller middle class, made up mostly of merchants, had much of their income cut off with embargoes on trade with the United States. They shared many of the same problems of the wealthy landowners.

Both wealthy and many middle-class Cubans fled to the United States, leaving the poorer and less-educated workers to administer the revolutionary government. The restructuring of the social order left a large vacancy to be filled by those loyal to the Cuban government. Outsiders have often wondered why Cuban nationals would put up with the dictates of Castro. It was their golden opportunity for advancement, however. Castro is still a hero to many, and with good reason.

LABOR

Although the average Cuban does not earn much money, there is almost no unemployment in Cuba. Nearly every Cuban has a job, but it is rarely possible for someone to choose the work he or she would like to do. All occupations are controlled by the Cuban government. A committee tries to match experience and training with positions ready to be filled.

Cuba's workforce includes both men and women. Before the revolution, most women stayed at home to take the lead in domestic and religious affairs. Children of the wealthy

A MIXTURE OF RACES

While Cubans have always stressed the importance of racial blending and tolerance, in practice physical distinctions have made a difference in Cuban society. About one-third of Cuba's 9 million people are considered black. Most are descendants of slaves brought from what now is Senegal, Gambia, Guinea, the Congo, and Nigeria. Others migrated from Haiti and the Bahamas, where their ancestors, too, were slaves. Many Cubans today are light-skinned and have blue eyes, but there are few Cuban-born pure-blooded Spanish people left on the island.

Although many of Cuba's heroes, such as Antonio Maceo, have been black, skin coloring has made a difference in obtaining good jobs in government and in the universities. The government's attempts at creating laws against discrimination were sometimes met with mixed emotions. Carlos Moré, the African-Cuban militant, felt that the absorption of blacks into the white community was the denial of black culture, which was humiliating to those who represented a large portion of the Cuban population. It was an admission that it was best to be white, and it denied pride in being black. Moré felt that blacks should have equal rights and equal respect, but that they should remain separate in their own communities. Not all agree with him. Increased educational opportunities have been important to blacks and have helped them attain higher standards of living. They do not feel they should keep to themselves in an all-black community.

were often educated abroad. For those who could not afford the luxury, children received their education at home. Today most mothers work outside the home. They are expected to join the labor force, the military, or the government, and to participate in volunteer organizations.

The main goal of the revolution was to eliminate social structures based on wealth and gender. Such changes mean an entirely new concept of the roles of men, women, and children. "The New Man," a term used by Che Guevara, which included both men and women, was someone dedicated to the goals of the revolution through hard work, both paid and unpaid.

The Federation of Cuban Women (Federación de Mujeres Cubanas) was created on August 23, 1960, with the job of uniting, organizing, and enabling all women over the age of fourteen to participate in the revolutionary process. One of its stated purposes was to free lower-class women from the gender-defined roles of live-in maids and prostitutes, which had been the only forms of employment open to them.

They have succeeded substantially. Now through advanced education and training, women from all backgrounds hold jobs in all ranks of the government.

Vilma Espin Guillois is an example of the changing role of women in Cuban society. She has served for more than twenty-six years as a Rebel Army coordinator, the highest-ranking woman in the Cuban government. In that job, she recruited other women to take on responsibilities outside the home. She was constantly on call to organize local community groups where women made important decisions about what construction projects should be undertaken to help their neighbors and themselves. They were often the ones who decided where schools and clinics should be located. Espin was an inspiration to many women, who would never have taken on such far-reaching responsibilities.

Women as well as men may find themselves in factory jobs. Little heavy industry exists, but some factories produce textiles, leather goods, chemicals, fertilizers, and construction materials; and all consumer goods are in short supply. People wait in long lines to buy everything from a bar of soap

Women participate in all levels of the Cuban economy from governing to the harvesting of sugarcane.

to shoes, which are made in Cuba. These are manufactured for export to bring in cash to bolster the economy.

Castro has tried to expand the industrialization of the country, but without sources of energy, not much progress has been made. Cuba has little oil and no natural gas or coal. Most of the nation's crude oil is still purchased from the former Soviet Union and from Venezuela and is refined on Cuban soil. It is an expensive drain on the economy.

HOMES THEN AND NOW

Between 1900 and 1959, the differences between economic classes were easy to see. Members of the upper, middle, and working classes living in the city had many conveniences such as electricity, running water, and plumbing. Most members of the lower class lived in rural areas where living conditions were quite primitive and lacked sanitation.

Today more Cubans are living in the cities. With transportation so difficult, people try to live close to their work, but there is a housing shortage in the cities. The government has built multistory apartment buildings in the cities, but rents are still too costly for some. Even for those with professional training, such as doctors, their government pay does not cover any luxuries. Pesos are in short supply.

WAGES

Most government employees are paid in pesos, the government currency. Because pesos do not buy much, the American dollar is highly sought after. At one time, however, Cubans could expect prison terms for holding "enemy" currency. In 1993 the government made it legal to own American dollars, yet there are few ways to earn that treasured cash.

Cabdrivers and gift shop owners are paid better than university-educated professors because they have access either to the American dollar or the convertible peso, which is now exchanged on a one-to-one value for tourists. Only Cubans providing certain services are allowed to charge for their work in convertible pesos. In 1997 the government established sixty skill categories for licensing, such as shoe repairing and beauty shop operators, which could be used by tourists. The foreign exchange for these services means that these specifically designated Cubans earn more than those paid directly by the government.

It is not uncommon to see medical doctors moonlighting as cabdrivers or opening their houses to paying visitors for meals. These newly opened, well-received restaurants are called *paladares*. In the center of Havana are some lovely old colonial homes. Many of them are in total disrepair, but others have been renovated. Families may open restaurants in their homes, so long as they serve no more than twelve people and limit their employees to four family members. This has saved the lives of many a family lucky enough to have a home in good condition.

FOOD

Ration cards are necessary to obtain food because there is a shortage of all but the most basic commodities. Even coffee and sugar, which are grown in quantity, are rationed because these crops are sent overseas to bring in cash to run the country.

Farmers' markets are now operating openly, with the growers marketing their own produce. By law, however, the prices have to be higher than government prices in a grocery store so as not to compete with state-owned stores. With prices high, local farmers are unable to sell much of what they do grow.

Fish has become a popular part of the diet. Cuban cooking is a mixture of traditional Spanish foods with Caribbean fruits and vegetables. A truly traditional meal would be a treat with chicken, beef, or pork being the main dish. Side helpings of fried plantains, a kind of banana, or sweet potatoes would be served. People love their copelia, fruit-flavored ice cream, but this would be a menu reserved only for certain festive occasions. Beans are still the staple diet.

Only two kinds of soda are available in Cuba. *La rubia* (red) is like ginger ale, and *la prieta* (dark) is Cuba's cola. Of course, though, the beverage that Cuba is most noted for is rum.

TRANSPORTATION

Food is not the only staple in short supply. Gasoline is also hard to come by. Few Cubans can afford a car, much less keep it filled with gasoline. Fin-tailed cars of the late 1950s are polished and kept in repair as much as possible, and a few boxy Russian-made Ladas continue to cruise the streets. Tires are so expensive that patches are now applied to patches.

Few Cubans can afford to own a car. Among those who do, older model American cars (left) and Russian-made Ladas (right) are common.

Bicycles are almost as numerous as in China. To get around Havana, Cuban engineers have built a giant hump-backed bus known as "the camel." Built to hold 320 passengers, the *camello* is said to be the largest bus in the world. There is no air conditioning, and complaints about the over-crowded, sweaty conditions have not made the *camello* the popular form of transportation expected.

When Russian money was available, Castro built an expressway between Havana and the coastal cities to the west. Today there is little intercity commuting and the highways are almost empty, except for an occasional donkey cart or tourist bus.

In 1984, again with funds from Russia, a railroad line was put into service connecting Havana and Santiago de Cuba, but it is used more for freight than for passenger service. Havana is the city most visited by tourists.

THE LOOK OF HAVANA

The majority of the buildings in Havana are decaying, but no amount of crumbling plaster or unpolished marble is able to diminish the grandeur of La Habana, as Cubans call it.

There is a remarkable variety of style, but a striking feature is that many of the buildings are made of heavy stone. Unlike structures in most tropical cities, which are built of wood, many older homes and public buildings in Havana are made of stone.

With additional help from UNESCO, a fund provided by the United Nations, the Cuban government has been restoring some of the buildings around the Plaza de Armas, a neo-classical marble monument. It was built in 1827 to house the paintings commissioned by the French artist Jean Baptiste Vermay depicting Cuba's early history.

Across the plaza is the sixteenth-century castle El Castillo de la Fuerza Real, built as a fort to protect the harbor. It is surrounded by a moat and a drawbridge, which is permanently lowered to permit visitors inside. It seems small and unimpressive today, but it must have provided protection when most needed, during the time Spain was fighting off contenders for supremacy of the seas around Cuba.

One of the most beautiful buildings in the old town is the Palacio de los Capitanes Generales, where the governors from Spain lived. Built in an ornate baroque style, it is fronted by a series of high arcades supported by ten marble columns, each topped with the Spanish coat of arms. Inside are beautiful stained-glass windows and rooms filled with gilded period furniture and artwork. Today it is a museum and gives a glimpse of the luxury once enjoyed by the wealthy.

TOURISM

Although the United States has cut off most visiting rights, travelers from other countries still enjoy these historic sights. Tourists make the hotels and restaurants profitable. Many

Massive stone columns, bricks, and carved inlays are found in many of Havana's public buildings.

Cubans would like to enjoy restaurants because no ration tickets are necessary, but few can afford restaurant prices.

Cuba's beautiful beaches and warm tropical weather lure many visitors. The problem is that few new hotels have been built, and there is not enough money to renovate what is left from the previous era of luxury. So, often tourists come out of curiosity, but they do not return because the quality of the service and facilities does not match what they could find elsewhere.

There is at least one notable exception. The Melia Cohiba in Havana was built in 1995 and can be considered a five-star resort. It has 22 stories and 347 rooms. A pool, elegant dining room, and meeting facilities are also available. Even for tourists, food is costly because much of it, especially meat, has to be imported.

Commercial airlines from Canada, Mexico, Spain, and a few other Western countries provide air service to Cuba. The United States discourages all travel to Cuba. Ironically, it is not against the law for U.S. citizens to travel to Cuba, but it is a violation of the U.S. government's 1963 Trading with the Enemy Act to spend money there. Occasional tourists and business personnel slip in by traveling to other exit cities outside the United States.

Castro is trying to encourage these excursion tours. He is also trying to attract conventions to fill up the vacant hotel rooms. Some say he is succeeding. For those who knew Cuba

An older hotel fronts the ocean. Although Castro encourages tourism, many visitors to Cuba are disappointed by the absence of modern accommodations.

before the revolution, there will be disappointment that renovation has not restored more older properties, but the sun and sand may lure others back.

"SOCIALISM OR DEATH"

Castro is putting out a welcome mat, but with reservations. As the Russian satellite countries began to move toward privatization of industry, Cuba under Fidel Castro has become more rigid than ever. His rallying cry is Socialism or Death.

Castro does not mean a firing squad, but he feels that Cubans will die of starvation if his form of government is not put into practice.

Castro challenges his people to show that Cubans, not Americans, can decide what is good for Cuba, and he scares them by preparing them for an impending invasion by the United States. His main prop is fear.

Castro instills pride in Cubans by pointing to the real achievements in the fields of free medical care, education, and social and economic equality. As far as can be ascertained, Castro is not corrupt. At one time several army officials were charged with trafficking drugs. Castro promptly dealt with the problem by calling in the firing squad.

An aging Castro in a stoic salute.

Castro is now in his seventies. Who will succeed him? His brother Raúl has been acting as head of the national police force, but most observers feel he does not have the leadership ability or the experience to take on the difficulties facing the country. No one else has been given a chance for on-the-job-training. There would certainly be a scramble for power if, for health reasons, Castro had to relinquish his role as dictator.

It has been more than five hundred years since Old World navigators discovered the New World. Cuba was one of the first lands to be entered in the written books of history, and it has had an important role in further pages of that history. While Cuba searches for its identity, it will no doubt continue to influence the world with its revolutionary form of government.

Facts About Cuba

The Government

Official name: Republic of Cuba
Type of government: Communist one-party system
Head of government: President of the Council of State, Fidel Castro
Legislature: National Assembly of People's Power

Governors and Presidents of Cuba:

1899–1902 Leonard Wood (U.S. military governor)
1902–1906 Tomás Estrada Palma (first president of the Republic of Cuba)
1906 William Howard Taft (provisional governor)
1906–1909 Charles Edward Magoon (provisional governor)
1909–1913 José Miguel Gómez
1913–1921 Mario García Menocal
1921–1925 Alfredo Zoyas
1925–1933 Gerardo Machado y Morales
1933– Carlos Manuel de Céspedes (provisional president)
1935–1936 José Barnet y Vinageras
1936 Miguel Mariano Gómez y Arias
1936–1940 Federico Laredo Brú
1940–1944 Fulgencio Batista y Zaldívar
1959 Manuel Urrutia Lleo (provisional president)
1959–1976 Osvaldo Dorticos Torrado
1976–Present Fidel Castro (formerly prime minister)

Political subdivisions: 14 provinces, 169 municipalities
Provinces and population figures:

Camagüey	664,566
Ciego de Avila	320,961
Cienfuegos	326,412
Ciudad de la Habana	1,924,886
Granma	739,335
Guantánamo	466,609
Holguín	911,034
Isla de la Juventud	57,879
La Habana	586,029
La Tunas	436,341
Matanzas	557,628

Pinar del Río	540,740
Sancti Spíritus	157,080
Santiago de Cuba	909,506
Villa Clara	764,743

PEOPLE

Population distribution: 72% urban, 28% rural

Annual estimated growth rate: 1.0%

Official language: Spanish

Literacy rate: 94% of adult population

Universities: 4

Hospital beds: 54,028

Physicians: 25,567

LAND AND RESOURCES

Land area: 746 miles (1,200 kilometers) long, with a median width of 62 miles (97 kilometers) and a maximum width of 125 miles (200 kilometers). The republic includes the Isla de la Juventud, formerly the Isle of Pines, and numerous keys and islets.

Highest elevation: Pico Turquino at 6,542 feet (1,994 meters)

Climate: Seasonal median temperatures range from 66 F (18 C) to 86 F (30 C). Rainy season from May to October, dry weather from December to April.

ECONOMY

Monetary unit: peso (100 centavos)

Weights and measures: metric system

Mineral resources: nickel, cobalt, iron, maganese, and copper

Chief crops and exports: sugar (principal cash crop; 85–95% of total foreign exchange earnings; industry employs nearly 500,000 workers), tobacco, and citrus crops.

FOREIGN TRADE

Imports: $3 billion (1991 est.)

Exports: $3.6 billion (1991 est.)

Principal trade partners: former USSR, China, Spain, Canada

TRANSPORTATION

Railroads: 7,862 miles (12,654 kilometers)

Roads: 10,378 miles (16,740 kilometers)

Major ports: 10

Major airfields: 3

FLAG

Three blue and two white horizontal stripes. Five-pointed white star on red triangle at side of hoist.

CHRONOLOGY

1492
Christopher Columbus discovers Cuba on October 27 and claims it for Spain

1511
Conquistador Diego de Velázquez builds a fort for the permanent protection of Cuba against other Euopean claims; Chief Hatuey is burned at the stake

1607
Havana established as capital, fortifes against pirate attacks

1728
University of Havana founded; Spanish authorize slave trade

1762
Havana falls to the British; free trade is established during brief occupation

1817
Agreement between Spain and England to end slave trade

1850
Economic depression; import duties are raised

1868
Cuba's first war for independence, the Ten Years' War, starts on October 11

1895
Cuba's second war for independence begins on February 24; José Julian Martí, the Cuban poet, writer, lawyer, and inspiration for the cause, is killed

1898
The Spanish-American War; the Treaty of Paris gives sovereign rights over Cuba to the United States

1901
Platt Amendment is added to Cuba's constitution, which limits the country's international powers and gives the

power to make decisions concerning Cuba's internal affairs to the United States; under the terms of the amendment, the United States is able to establish the Guantánamo naval base (1903)

1906
Revolution occurs in August; U.S. troops intervene

1933
Military coup puts Fulgencio Batista in power; Ramón Gran San Martín acts as provisional president

1938
Communist Party recognized in Cuba as legal organization

1940
The democratic constitution of Cuba is adopted

1952
Batista seizes power on March 10; puts an end to the constitution

1953
Fidel Castro and followers lead a futile attack on army barracks near Santiago on July 26; survivors are sentenced to prison; Batista grants amnesty; Castro heads for Mexico

1958
Fidel Castro returns to Cuba and launches attacks on Batista's troops from rebel headquarters in the mountains of the Sierra Maestra

1959
Rebels take control; Batista flees the country; Castro arrives in Havana and enacts Agrarian Reform Law; he travels to Washington, D.C., for meeting with congressional representatives; refuses aid if restrictions are attached

1960
Cuba establishes relations with the Soviet Union and nationalizes properties owned by North American companies

1961
In April, an invasion by Cuban expatriates fails at the Bay of Pigs

1970
Sugar harvest disaster; economy fails

1975
Cuba sends combat troops to help Angola fight for liberation from Portugal

1980
Over 125,000 Cubans immigrate by boat to the United States

1998
Pope John Paul II and other dignitaries visit Cuba; some concessions are made toward religious freedom

NOTES

CHAPTER 1: DISCOVERY

1. Quoted in Byron Williams, *Cuba: The Continuing Revolution.* New York: Parents' Magazine Press, 1969, p. 14.

2. Quoted in Stephen Williams, *Cuba: The Land, the History, the People, the Culture.* Philadelphia: Running Press, 1994, p. 12.

CHAPTER 3: SPANISH CONTROL

3. Quoted in Byron Williams, *Cuba*, p. 69.

4. Quoted in Louis A. Perez Jr., *Cuba: Between Reform and Revolution.* New York: Oxford University Press, 1988, p. 166.

5. Quoted in Geoff Simons, *Cuba: From Conquistador to Castro.* New York: St. Martin's Press, 1996, p. 179.

CHAPTER 4: FREE AT LAST

6. Quoted in Simons, *Cuba*, p. 154.

CHAPTER 5: CASTRO HAS HIS WAY

7. Quoted in Byron Williams, *Cuba*, p. 86.

8. Quoted in Lester Sobel, ed., *Castro's Cuba in the 1970s.* New York: Facts On File, 1978, p. 98.

9. Quoted in Byron Williams, *Cuba*, p. 193.

10. Quoted in Carmelo Mesa-Lago, ed., *Cuba After the Cold War.* Pittsburgh: University of Pittsburgh Press, 1993, p. 6.

CHAPTER 6: THE CULTURE OF CUBA

11. Quoted in Brook Larmer and Rod Nordland, "Preaching to the Masses," *Newsweek*, February 2, 1998, p. 57.

12. Quoted in Larmer and Nordland, "Preaching to the Masses," p. 57.

13. Quoted in Larmer and Nordland, "Preaching to the Masses," p. 57.

14. Henry Schroeder, journalist representing the Wisconsin Newspaper Association, interviewed by the author.

15. Henry Schroeder, interviewed by the author.

SUGGESTIONS FOR FURTHER READING

Clifford Crouch, *Cuba: People and Places of the World.* New York: Chelsea House, 1991. A general review of the culture of the Cuban people.

Karen Jacobsen, *Cuba.* Chicago: Childrens Press, 1990. A book for younger readers about everyday life in Cuba.

Douglas Keller, *Ernesto "Che" Guevara.* New York: Chelsea House, 1989. A biography that documents Guevara's life as a child as well as his revolutionary activities.

Keith Lye, *Take a Trip to Cuba.* New York: Franklin Watts, 1987. Describes a trip to Cuba for young readers.

Jay Mallin, *Ernesto "Che" Guevara: Modern Revolutionary, Guerrilla Theorist.* Charlotteville, NY: SamHar Press, 1973. Documents the life of a young man searching for causes.

Earle Rice Jr., *The Cuban Revolution.* San Diego: Lucent Books, 1995. A well-documented account of the changes in Cuba's government in the twentieth century.

Ana Maria B. Vázquez and Rosa E. Casas, *Cuba.* Chicago: Childrens Press, 1987. A volume in the Enchantment of the World series, giving the history, geography, economics, and culture of Cuba.

Margot Williams and Josephine McSweeney, *Cuba from Columbus to Castro.* New York: Julian Messner, 1982. A complete history of Cuba, with emphasis on people who influenced events.

WORKS CONSULTED

BOOKS

Haynes Bonner Johnson, *The Bay of Pigs: The Leaders' Story of Brigade 2506*. New York: W. W. Norton 1964. A detailed personal account of the invasion at the Bay of Pigs.

Carmelo Mesa-Lago, ed., *Cuba After the Cold War*. Pittsburgh: University of Pittsburgh Press, 1993. Covers the economic and political changes since the Soviet Union's withdrawal of support from Cuba.

Louis A. Perez Jr., *Cuba: Between Reform and Revolution*. New York: Oxford University Press, 1988. Uses documented statistics to show why there have been so many changes in the Cuban government.

James D. Rudolph, ed., *Cuba, a Country Study*. 3rd ed. Washington, DC: Headquarters, Dept. of the Army; U.S. GPO, 1985. History, geography, and politics covered in detail.

Geoff Simons, *Cuba: From Conquistador to Castro*. New York: St. Martin's Press, 1996. Covers Cuba's history from the Spanish period to Castro's regime.

Lester Sobel, ed., *Castro's Cuba in the 1970s*. New York: Facts On File, 1978. Particularly details Castro's dealings with the Soviet Union at this time.

David Stanley, *Cuba: A Lonely Planet Travel Survival Kit*. Oakland, CA: Lonely Planet, 1997. A description of Cuba today from a traveler's perspective.

Byron Williams, *Cuba: The Continuing Revolution*. New York: Parents' Magazine Press, 1969. An account of the early fights for freedom.

Stephen Williams, *Cuba: The Land, the History, the People, the Culture*. Philadelphia: Running Press, 1994. Uses beautiful pictures to illustrate its theme.

Peter Wood and the Editors of Time-Life Books, *The Spanish Main*. Alexandria, VA: Time-Life Books, 1979. A history of the early conquest of the New World.

PERIODICALS

"Brother Fidel and the Women of Cuba," *Economist*, February 18, 1998.

Alexander Cockburn, "To Swine," *Nation*, March 9, 1998.

Eduardo Costa, "Report from Havana—The Installation Biennial," *Art in America*, March 1998.

"The Cost of Castro," *Forbes*, March 2, 1998.

Charles Lane, "Castro Inconvertible," *New Republic*, February 9, 1998.

Brook Larmer and Rod Nordland, "Preaching to the Masses," *Newsweek*, February 2, 1998.

Steve Marantz, "Dealing with Defects," *Sporting News*, January 22, 1996.

Robert Plunket, "Havana Heyday," *Life*, March 1993.

S. L. Price, "The Best Little Sports Machine in the World," *Sports Illustrated*, May 15, 1995.

Julia Reed, "Our Girl in Havana," *Vogue*, September 1994.

"The Squeeze Is On: Cuba Policy," *Economist*, March 21, 1998.

Anthony Stevens-Arroyo, "Papal Politics for Cuba," *Nation*, March 2, 1998.

INDEX

abortion, 70
Africa, 33, 65, 70
Agrarian Reform Law, 57
Agrupación Católica University, 53
Alicia Alonso National School of Ballet, 74
almonds, 24
Alonso, Martín, 13
Alviza, Lidzie, 75
American dollar, 88
American Revolutionary War, 31
Angola, 65
Antilles, 13
Arawaks. *See* Tainos
Arnez, Desi, 73
art of Cuba, 75–76
avocados, 24

B-26 bombers, 59
Bahamas, 86
ballet, 74
bananas, 24
baseball, 76–78
bata criolla, 74
batey, 77
Batista y Zaldívar, Fulgencio, 7, 43–45, 49–52, 55, 57, 60, 73, 79
Bayamo, 34–35
Bay of Pigs, 59–61
beans, 19, 24, 52, 89
beef, 89
béisbol, 77
bicycles, 90
birds, 20, 24
Bizet, Georges, 73
black population of Cuba, 86
black virgins, 71
boat people, 65–66
Bolivia, 83
bongo drums, 73
boxing, 76
Brigade 2506, 60
buildings of Havana, 90–91
butterfly jasmine, 21

cabdrivers, 88
cacique, 11, 14, 16
Camagüey province, 51
camello, 90
Canada, 92
Canary Islands, 9
canoes, 14

capitalism, 69, 79
Carboneys, 14
Carmen (opera), 73
Carnival, 71–72
cars, 89–90
Carter, Jimmy, 66
cassava bread, 14
Castro Díaz-Balart, Fidel, 46
Castro, Fidel
   develops five-point program, 65
   as leader of Cuban Revolution, 7
   overthrows dictator Batista, 44–47, 49–51
   response to rule of, 8
   slogan of, 68, 93
   on the United States, 58, 69, 79
   views of, about democracy, 56
Castro, Raúl, 44, 51, 93
Catholic Church, 34, 70
cattle, 25–27, 54
caves, 14, 20
cays, 18
Central America, 65
cha-cha, 73
Chartrand, Esteban, 76
cheese, 26
chemicals, 87
chess, 77
chicken, 89
children in Cuba, 33, 85–86
chivatos, 51
Christianity, 13
chromate, 26
Cienfuego, Camilo, 51
cigarettes, 25
cigars, 24–25
citrus, 19–20
claves, 73
climate of Cuba, 22
Clinton, Bill, 84
cobalt, 26
cockfighting, 78
coconuts, 24
coffee, 24, 89
Cold War, 61
Colegio de Belen, 46
Columbus, Christopher, 9–13, 15
Comites de Defensiva de la Revolución, 57
communism, 44, 55, 58, 61, 68–69, 72, 79
Communist Party, 83

conga, 73–74
Congo, 86
constitutions of Cuba, 56, 65
copelia, 89
coral, 15, 18
corn, 14, 19, 24
Costa Rica, 84
cotton, 14
Council for Mutual Assistance, 65
countess of Merlin, 75
criollos, 8
crocodiles, 20
crops, 17, 19–20, 42, 80
crude oil, 88
crude steel, 26
Cuba: The Land, the History, the People, the Culture (Williams), 65
Cuba from Conquistador to Castro (Simons), 45
Cuban bee hummingbird, 20
Cuban crocodile, 20
Cuban Revolution, 46, 48, 57
Cuban Revolutionary Council, 60–61
Cuban Revolutionary Party, 36
Cueva de Bellamar, 20
Cueva de los Indios, 20
Cugat, Xavier, 73
culture of Cuba, 69–79
currency of Cuba, 88
cycling, 77
Czechoslovakia, 61, 79

dairy products, 26
dancing, 73
Day of Liberation, 73
deer, 14, 20
deities, 70–71
democracy, 56
destiny of humans, 71
Diaz-Balart, Mírta, 46
diphtheria, 83
discovery of Cuba, 9–17
diving, 77
dogs, 17
Dominican Republic, 12
dominoes, 77
Dorticos Torrado, Osvaldo, 55
Dos Ríos, 36
dramas, 74
droughts, 23
drums, 73

earthquakes, 18
ebony, 21
economy of Cuba, 44, 61, 65, 88
education, 34, 53, 80–83, 86
Eisenhower, Dwight D., 51, 55–58
El Castillo de la Fuerza Real, 91
electric power, 19, 54
El Morro, 30, 40–41
England, 28
Escobar, Vicente, 76

Espin Guillois, Vilma, 87
Estefan, Gloria, 73
Estrada Palma, Tomás, 40
Ethiopia, 65
expressways, 90

factories, 86–87
farmers' markets, 89
Federación de Mujeres Cubanas, 86
Federation of Cuban Women, 86
fertilizers, 87
film, 74
Finlay, Carlos, 23
fish, 14, 21, 89
five-point program, 65
flamenco dancers, 73
Florida, 15, 18, 28, 31
food rationing, 61, 89
forecasting the weather, 14
France, 29, 31
freedom of speech, 34
fruit, 14
Future Farmers of America, 83

Gambia, 86
gambling, 45, 78
gasoline, 89
glasnost, 67
gods, 70–71
gold, 11–12, 15–17, 20, 23, 27
Gómez de Avellaneda, Gertrudis, 75
Gómez y Báez, Máximo, 36
Gorbachev, Mikhail, 67
Granma, 47, 49, 52, 78
Grau Sau Martín, Ramón, 43
Great Depression, 43
Grenada, 66
guajiros, 33
Guantánamo, 42, 64, 77
guarapo, 23
guavas, 24
Guevara, Ernesto "Che", 45, 47–48, 50–51, 86
Guinea, 86
guiro, 73
Gulf of Mexico, 6, 15
Gulf Stream, 15

"Habanera," 73
Haiti, 12, 31–32, 86
hammocks, 14
harbors, 19
harpoons, 14
Hautey, 16–17
Havana
    attack of battleship *Maine* in, 38–39
    buildings of, 90–91
    discovery of harbor of, 15
    fortification of, 30
    gambling in, 45
    May Day celebration in, 72
    music scene of, 73

pirates rob ships in, 27, 29
protesters seek political asylum in, 66
reduction of mosquitoes in, 23
siege of, by England, 28
spiritual patron of, 71
theaters in, 74
tourism and, 6
transportation in, 90
workers call general strike in, 43
Havana Biennial Art Show, 75
Havana Psychiatric Hospital, 84
Havana Symphony Orchestra, 74
health care, 83–84
Hemingway, Ernest, 75
high jump, 76
Hispaniola, 12, 15–16
History Will Absolve Me (Castro), 44
holidays in Cuba, 71–73
hospitals, 83–84
hotels, 91–92
housing in Cuba, 88
humidity, 22
Hungary, 79
hurricanes, 22–23, 61
hygiene, 84

ice cream, 89
immigration, 28, 66
income of families in Cuba, 52
independence of Cuba, 31–32, 34
Indians, 12–13, 15, 17
Institute of Cinematographic Art and Industry, 74
International Workers' Day, 73
intestinal parasites, 53
Isla de la Juventud, 18
Isle of Pines, 18, 44
Italy, 77

Jamaica, 18
Japan, 26, 77–78
Jefferson, Thomas, 6
John Paul II, Pope, 69–70, 84

Kennedy, John F., 60, 62–63
Key West, 18
Khan, Kublai, 11
Khrushchev, Nikita, 63–64

labor in Cuba, 85–88
Ladas, 89–90
La Habana. *See* Havana
Lake Hanabanilla, 19
Lam, Wilfredo, 76
languages of Cuba, 84
Lansky, Meyer, 45
la prieta, 89
La Punta, 30
la rubia, 89
lead, 26
leather, 26, 87

lectores de tabaquería, 25
Ledon, Ramon, 77
libraries, 28
life expectancy in Cuba, 83
literacy rate of Cuba, 80
literature of Cuba, 74–75
López, Narcisco, 32, 34
Louisiana, 31
Lucimi, 58, 70

Maceo y Grajales, Antonio, 36–37, 86
Machado y Morales, Gerardo, 43
magazines, 57
magic spells, 71
mahogany, 21, 27
maids, 87
Maine, 38–39
malaria, 21, 23, 83
Malia Cohiba, 92
mambo, 73
mangroves, 19
Manuel de Céspedes, Carlos, 34
Manzanillo, 47, 49
maracas, 73
Mardi Gras, 71
Mariel, 66
marriage, 33
Martí, José Julian, 35–36, 40, 75
Marx, Karl, 61
Matahambre mines, 26
May Day, 72
measles, 83
meat, 52
medical supplies in Cuba, 84
melado, 22
men-of-war, 27
mental patients, 84
Mesa, Victor, 76
mestizos, 8
Mexico, 18, 27, 92
Miami Sound Machine, 73
Middle East, 65
milk, 26
minerals, 26
mines, 26, 54
Ministry of Public Health, 83
missile crisis, 61–64
Mississippi River, 31
Moncada, 44, 51
Monroe Doctrine, 32
Monroe, James, 32
Montmartyre casino, 45
Moré, Carlos, 86
mortality rate of Cuba, 83
mosquitoes, 21, 23, 41
Mozambique, 65
mulattos, 8
museums, 75
music of Cuba, 73–74

national anthem of Cuba, 34–35
National City Bank, 42

New Orleans, 31, 71
New World, 10
newspapers, 23, 28, 57, 78–79
nickel, 26
Nigeria, 86
Nimitz-class aircraft carriers, 13
Niña, 9, 13
Nixon, Richard, 56
Nobel Prize, 75
North Korea, 68
novels, 75
Núñez, Raúl, 70

OAS. *See* Organization of American States
Ocampo, Sebastian de, 14–15
ocean currents, 15
O'Farill, Arturo "Chico", 73
oil refining, 54
Old Man and the Sea, The (Hemingway), 75
Olifi, 71
Olney, Richard, 37
Olympics, 76, 78
operas, 73–74
Organización de Pioneras José Martí, 83
Organization of American States (OAS), 61, 63
Organization of Eastern Caribbean States, 66
organized crime, 45
Oriente province, 46

Palacio de los Capitanes Generales, 91
paladars, 89
Pan American Games, 76
Party of the Socialist Revolution, 61
peninsulares, 30–31
perestroika, 67
Peréz de Angulo, 29
Peru, 27
pesos, 88
photography, 75
Pico Turquino, 50
Pinar del Río, 26
Pinta, 9, 13
Pinzón, Martín Alonso, 13
Pinzón, Vincente Yáñez, 13
pioneers, 83
pirates, 27, 29, 33
plantains, 89
Platt Amendment, 40–41
plays, 74
Plaza de Armas, 91
Plaza de Revolución, 72
poetry, 75
polio, 83
political asylum, 66
Polo, Marco, 9
Popular Socialist Party, 56–57
population of Cuba, 6, 86

pork, 89
postal service, 28
posters, 76
professors, 88
prostitutes, 87
public library, 28
pythons, 20

rabbits, 14, 20
racial tolerance, 86
radio programming, 57
railroads, 54, 90
rainy season, 22
rationing food, 61, 89
Rayos y Soles de Bolívar, 32
Reagan, Ronald, 66
Rebel Army, 57, 87
Reed, Walter, 23
religions of Cuba, 69–71
rents, 57
restaurants, 89, 91–92
rice, 19, 24, 52
rivers, 19
Roig, Gonzalo, 74
Roman Catholics, 69
Roosevelt, Theodore, 39
Rough Riders, 39
rowing, 77
Royal Bank of Canada, 42
rugby, 77
rum, 23, 27, 89
rumba, 73–74

sailing, 77
Saint Barbara, 70–71
sanitation, 41, 54, 88
San Juan Hill, 39
San Salvador, 9–10
Santa María, 9, 12–13
Santeria, 70–71
Santiago de Cuba, 29, 39, 44, 47, 51, 90
Saturday Evening Post, 45
Savedra, Lázaro, 75
sculpture, 75–76
sea life, 21
Senegal, 86
shoe industry, 26
Sicre, Juana José, 76
Sierra Maestra, 18, 50
Simons, Geoff, 45
sinkholes, 20
slavery, 31–35, 72, 75, 86
snakes, 20
soccer, 77
Socialism or Death slogan, 68, 93
soda, 89
Sores, Jacques de, 29
South America, 65
Soviet Union, 61–68, 88
Spain
    air service to Cuba from, 92

conquest of Cuba by, 17
control of Cuba by, 27–39
discovery of Cuba by, 9–17
language of, 84
wars with France, 29
Spanish Main, 27
sports, 76–78
Sports Illustrated, 76
squirrels, 14, 20
state ownership of land, 57
steel, 26
stool pigeons, 51
sugar
celebrations for harvest of, 72
as Cuba's cash crop, 22–23, 42, 61
price of, during Great Depression, 43
as primary ingredient for making rum, 27
production of
Castro attempts to break record tonnage of, 64
effects of prices on, 53
effects of weather on, 61
harvests and, 87
workers in factory, 85
purchases of, canceled by United States, 58
rationing of, 89
use of slaves to grow crops of, 33
sugar beets, 42
Summer Olympics, 76, 78
swamplands, 19
sweet potatoes, 89
swimming, 77

Tainos, 13–14, 25, 77
taxes, 43, 57
Teatro Nacional, 74
Teatro Tacón, 28
telephones, 54
television programming, 57
temperatures in Cuba, 21
Ten Years' War, 34–39
textiles, 87
theaters, 28, 74
tires, 89
tobacco, 17, 20, 24–25
tools, 14
torcedores, 25
tourism, 45, 88, 90–93
Toussaint-Louverture, 31
track-and-field events, 77
trade embargo, 58, 69, 84
trade winds, 15
Trading with the Enemy Act, 92
transportation, 89–90
Triana, Rodrigo de, 9
tropical storms, 22
tuberculosis, 53
typhus, 53

unemployment, 85
UNESCO, 90

United Nations, 64
United States
allows Cubans to immigrate, 66
annexation of Cuba to, 32
attack of battleship *Maine* and, 38–39
ban on tourism in Cuba by, 91–92
control of industries in Cuba, 54
diplomatic relations with Cuba and, 55–58
enters World War II, 44
involvement in Bay of Pigs incident, 59–61
military intervention in Cuba, 40–41
missile crisis and, 61–64
possible war between Spain and, 31
sympathy toward Cuba, 37
trade embargo against Cuba, 58, 69, 84
University of Havana, 28, 41, 46, 82
Urrutia Lleo, Manuel, 52–53, 55
U.S. Foreign Relations Committee, 55
U.S. Navy, 63
USSR. *See* Soviet Union
utilities, 54, 57

valla, 78
Velázquez, Diego, 16
Venezuela, 88
Vermay, Jean Baptiste, 91
Villaverde, Cirilo, 74–75
Virgin Mary, 71
Virgin of Regia, 71
volleyball, 76

wages, 88–89
War of Independence Day, 73
weather forecasting, 14
West Indian ebony, 20
West Indies, 10
Weyer y Nicolau, Valeriano, 36
whooping cough, 83
wildcats, 14, 24
Williams, Stephen, 65
women in Cuba, 85–88
World War I, 42
World War II, 44
writers of Cuba, 74–75

yellow fever, 21, 23, 41
YMCA, 83
Yucatán Peninsula, 15, 18
YWCA, 83

Zanjón, Treaty of, 28, 34
Zapata rail, 20
Zapata Swamp, 20–21
Zapata wren, 20
zapateo, 73
zinc, 26

PICTURE CREDITS

Cover photo: © Hazel Hankin/Impact Visuals
AP/Wide World Photos, 46, 47, 51, 63, 64, 70, 71, 73, 78, 90
Archive Photos, 31, 41, 49, 92
Canadian Press Photo/AP Wide World Photos, 72
Corbis-Bettmann, 11, 12, 17, 33, 37, 75
European Photo/FPG International, 43, 56
FPG International, 21, 22, 43, 53
Keystone View Company/FPG International, 85
Miki Kratsman/Corbis-Bettmann, 67
Library of Congress, 10, 23 (top), 28, 38, 62
North Wind Picture Archives, 29, 61
PhotoDisc, 30, 81, 82, 91
Popperfoto/Archive Photos, 25
Reuters/Corbis-Bettmann, 68
Reuters/Rafael Perez/Archive Photos, 8, 93
Reuters/Enrique Shore/Archive Photos, 13
United Nations, 48
UPI/Corbis-Bettmann, 23 (bottom), 36, 42, 54, 57, 87

ABOUT THE AUTHOR

Mary Virginia Fox is the author of more than forty books for young readers. As a freelance writer, her work has also appeared in newspapers and magazines. She and her husband lived in the Philippines, Iran, Colombia, South America, and Tunisia for several months at a time, where she continued her writing. She is a graduate of Northwestern University and currently lives in Madison, Wisconsin. She is an instructor for the Institute of Children's Literature.